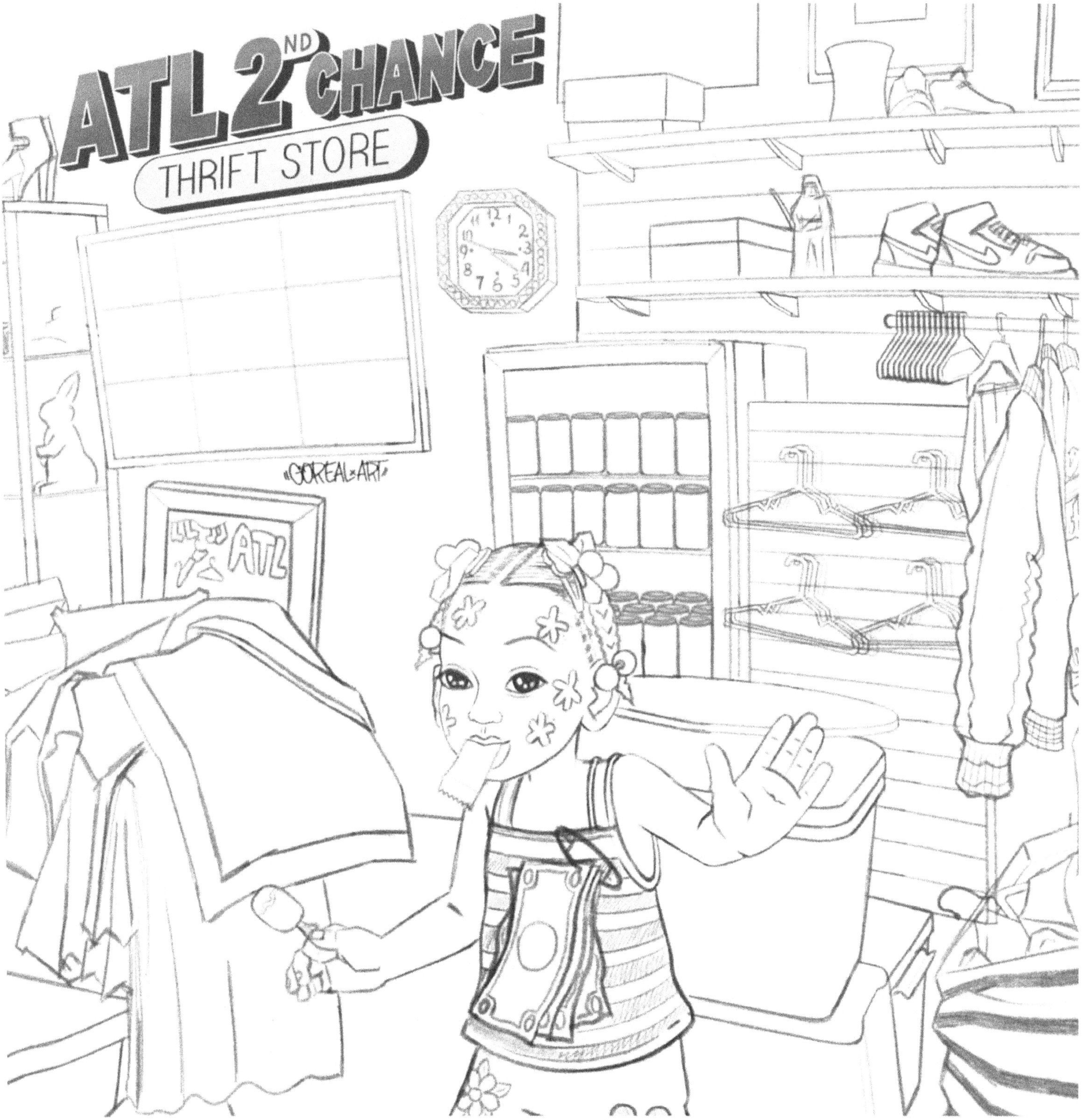
ATL 2ND CHANCE
THRIFT STORE
GOREAL ART
ATL

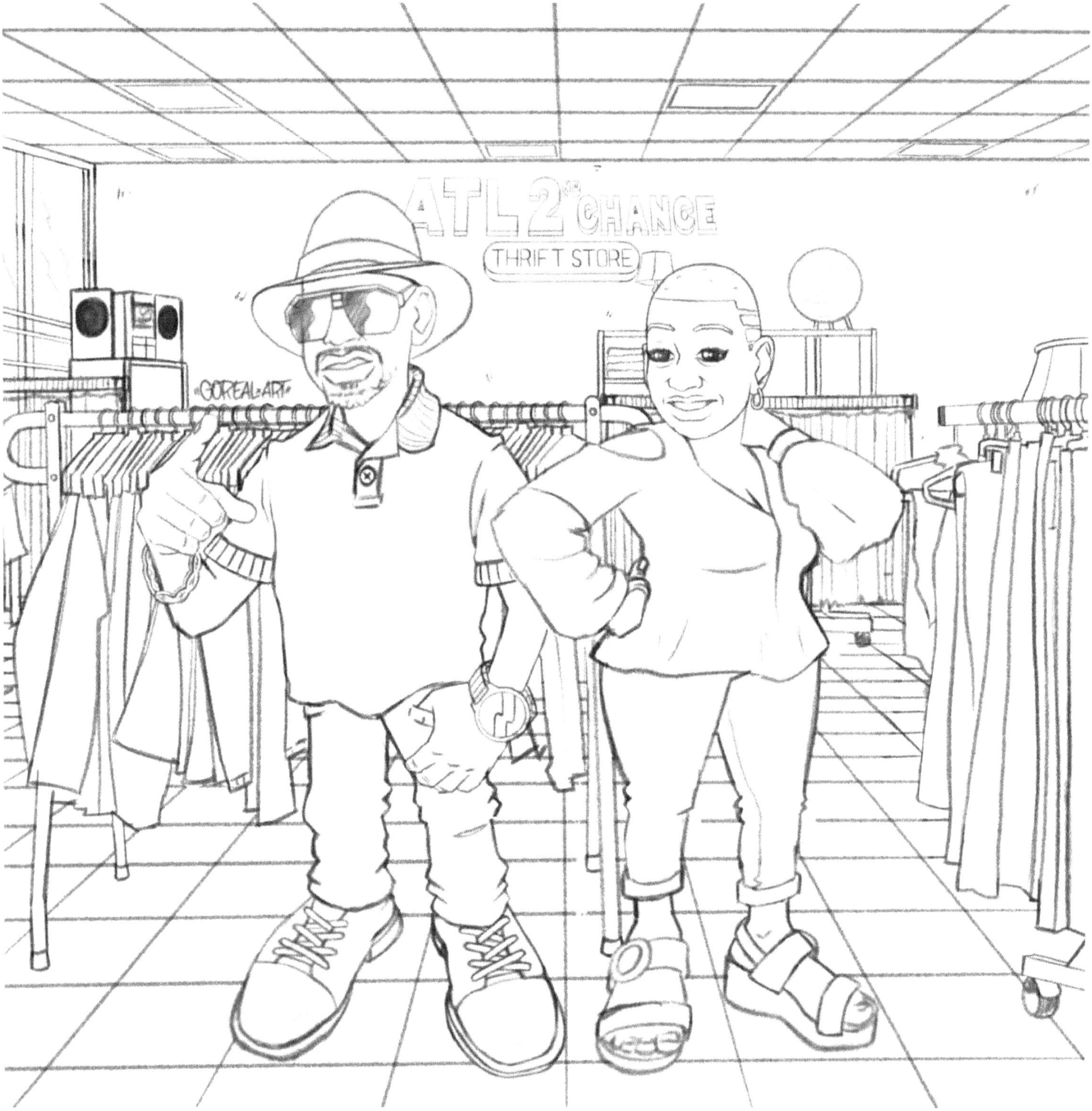
ATL 2nd CHANCE
THRIFT STORE
GOREAL ART

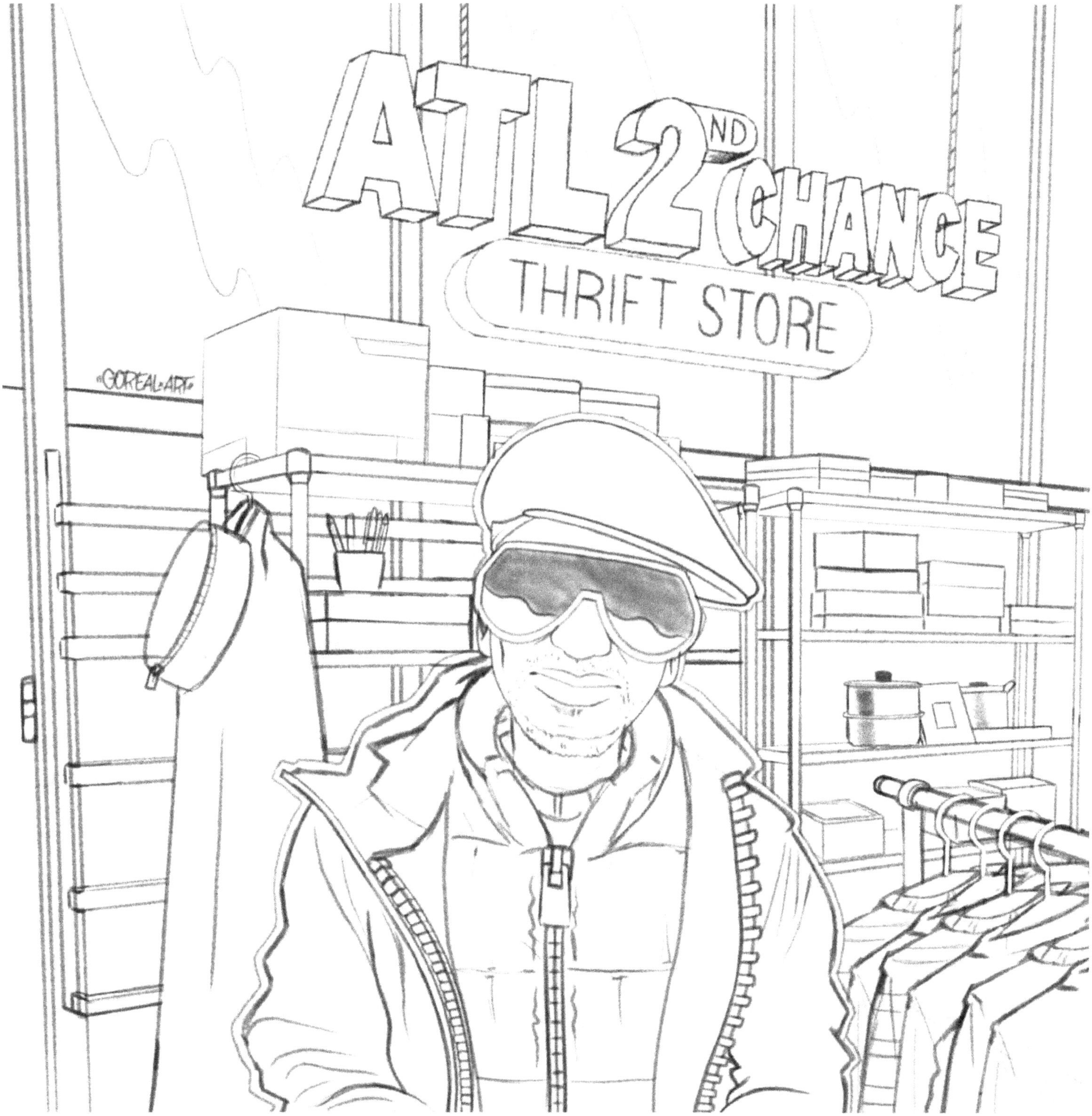
ATL 2ND CHANCE
THRIFT STORE
@GOREAL.ART

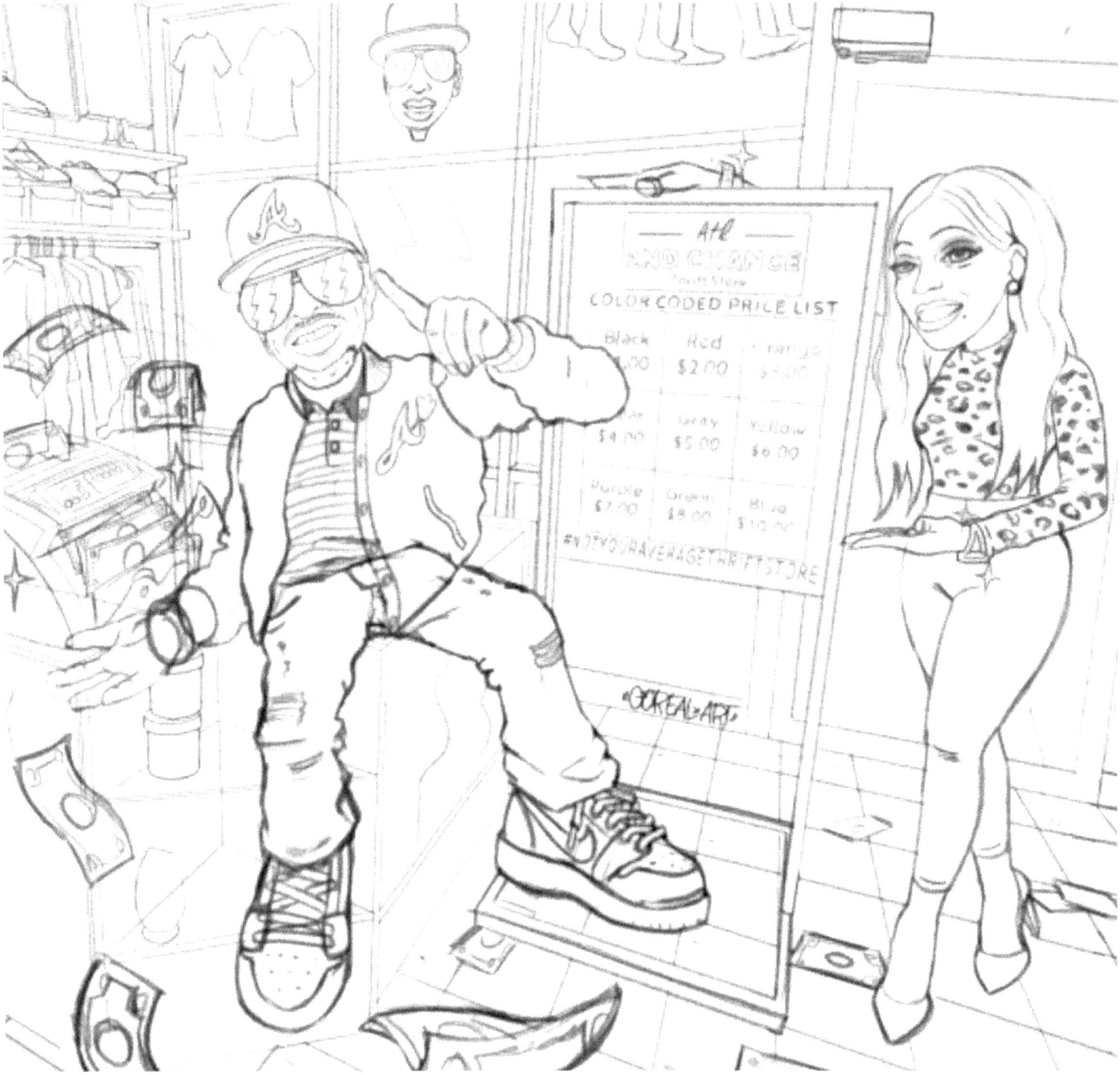

Atl
2ND CHANGE
Thrift Store
COLOR CODED PRICE LIST
Black
Red
$2.00
Gray
$5.00
Yellow
$6.00
Purple
$7.00
Green
Blue
#NOTYOURAVERAGETHRIFTSTORE

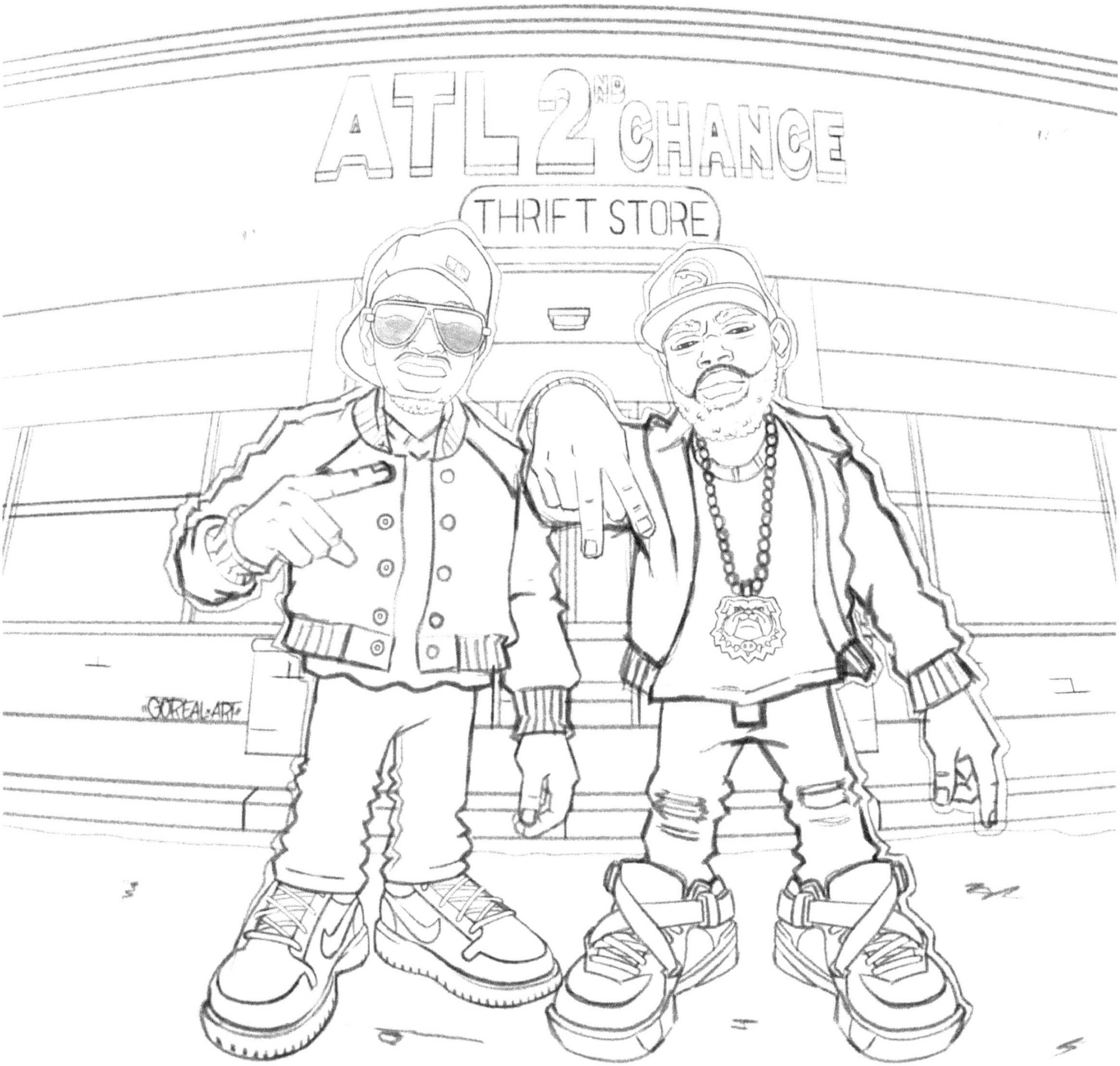
ATL 2ND CHANCE
THRIFT STORE
GOREAL ART

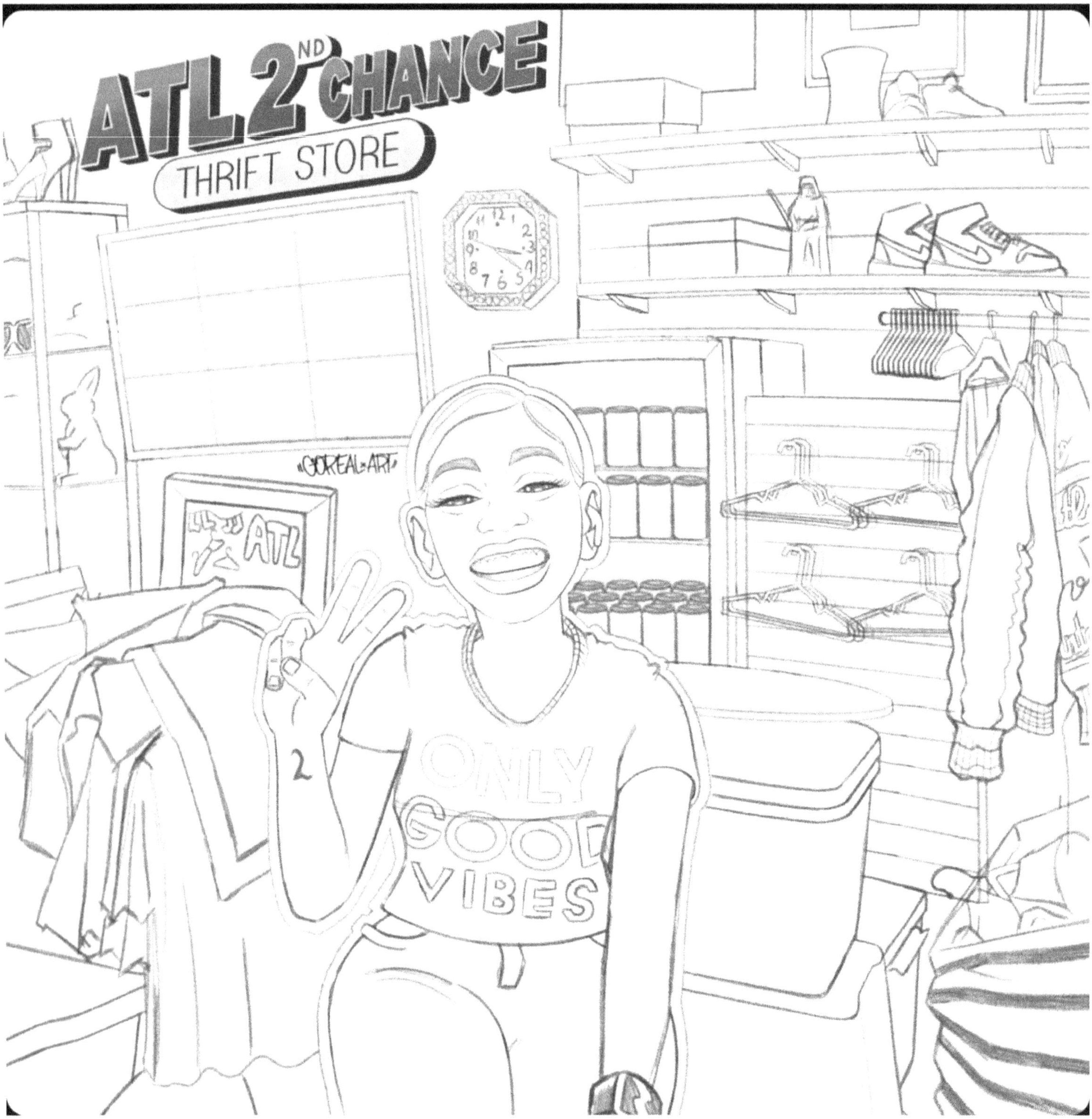
ATL 2ND CHANCE
THRIFT STORE
ATL
ONLY
GOOD
VIBES
2

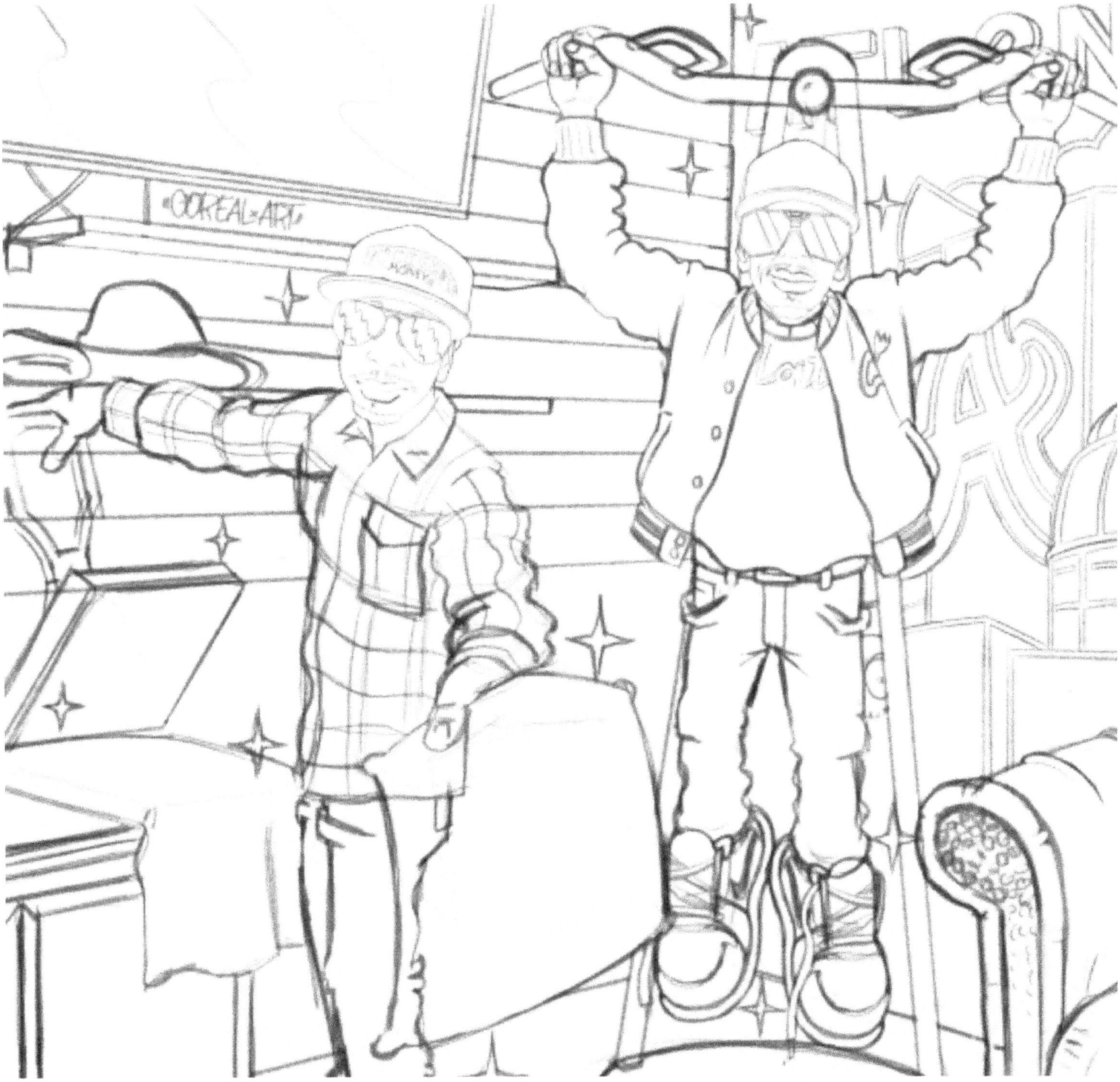
OOREAL ART

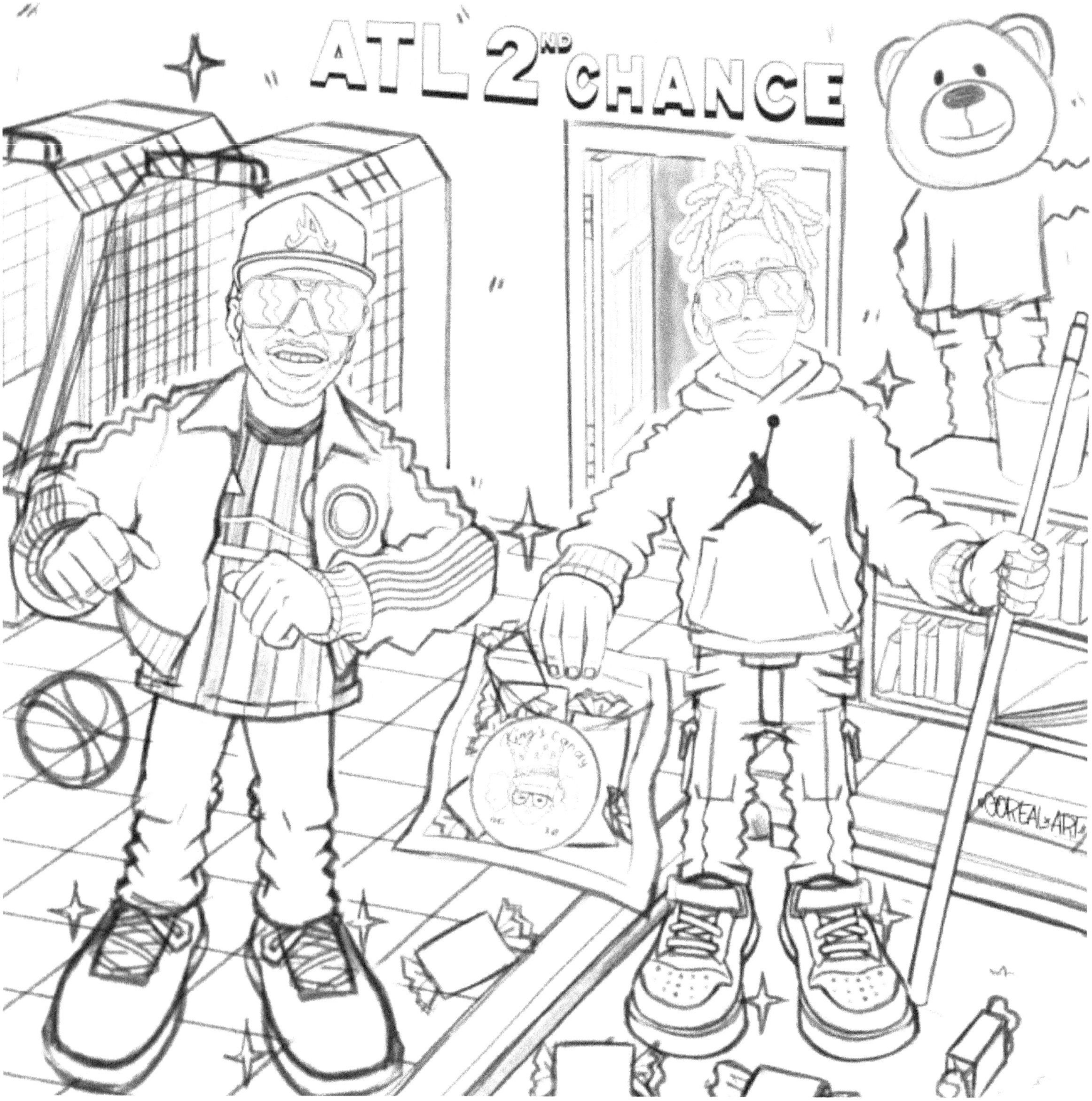
ATL 2ND CHANCE
King's Candy
GOREAL ART

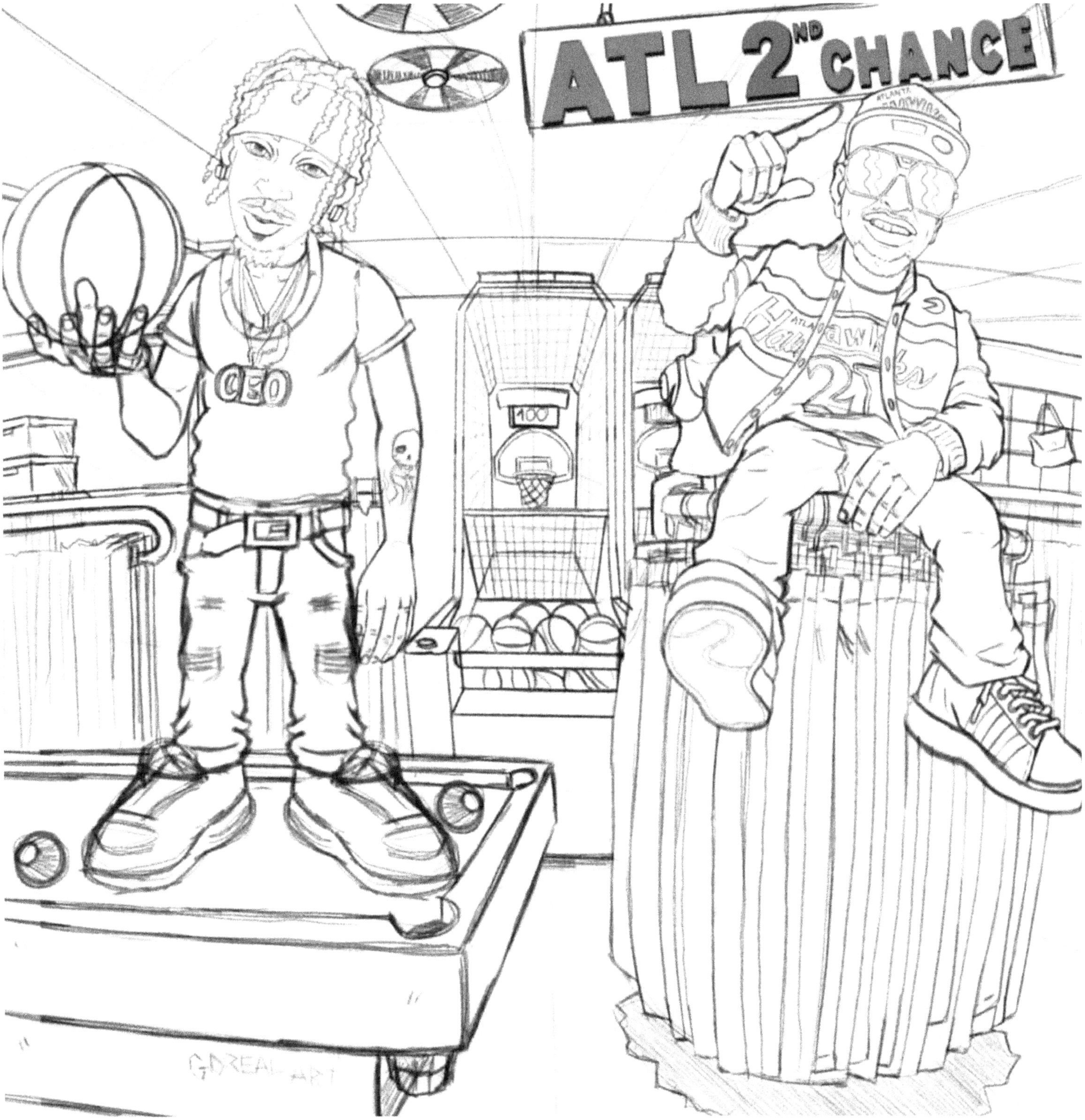
ATL 2ND CHANCE
CEO
100

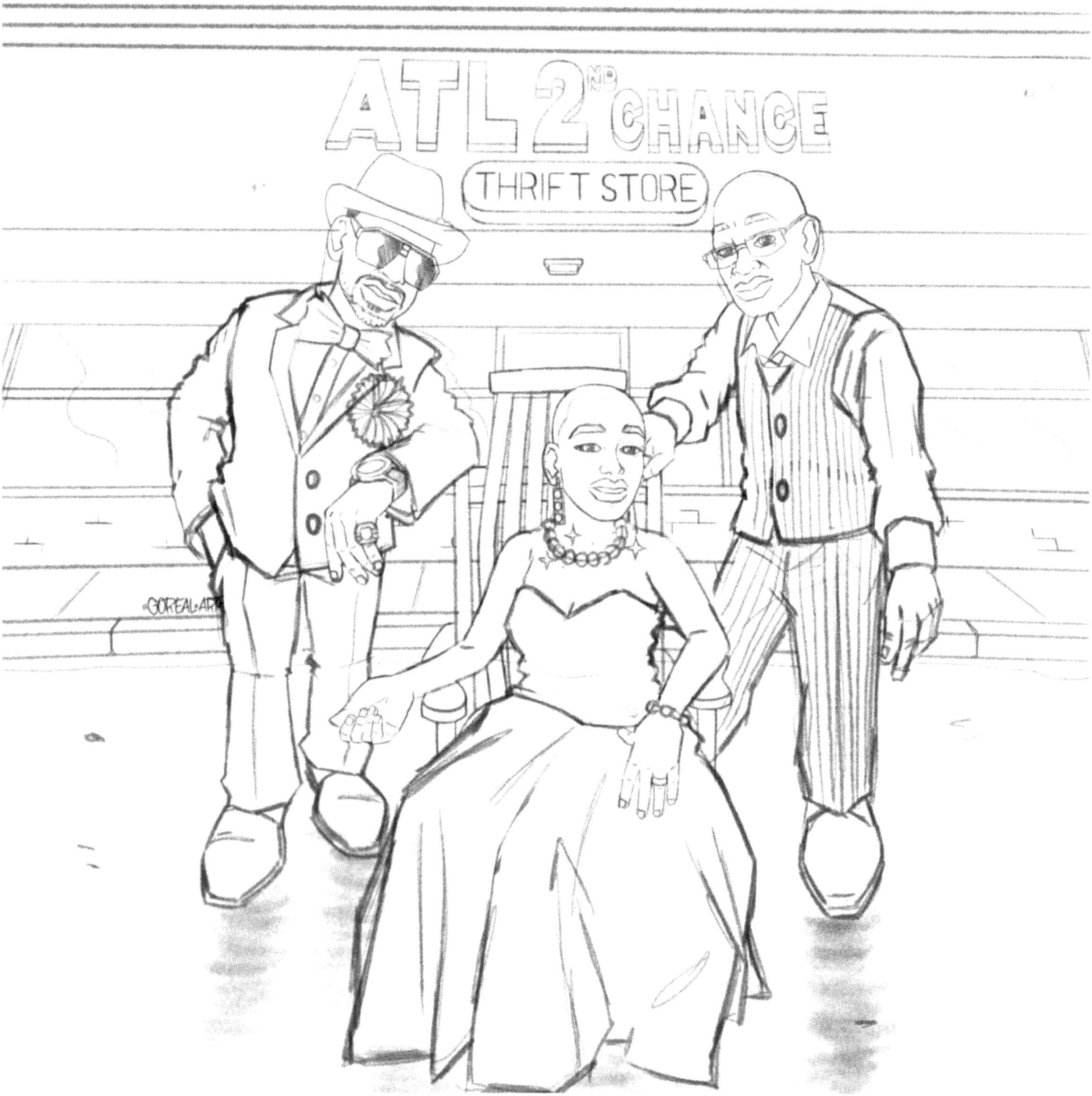
ATL 2ND CHANCE
THRIFT STORE

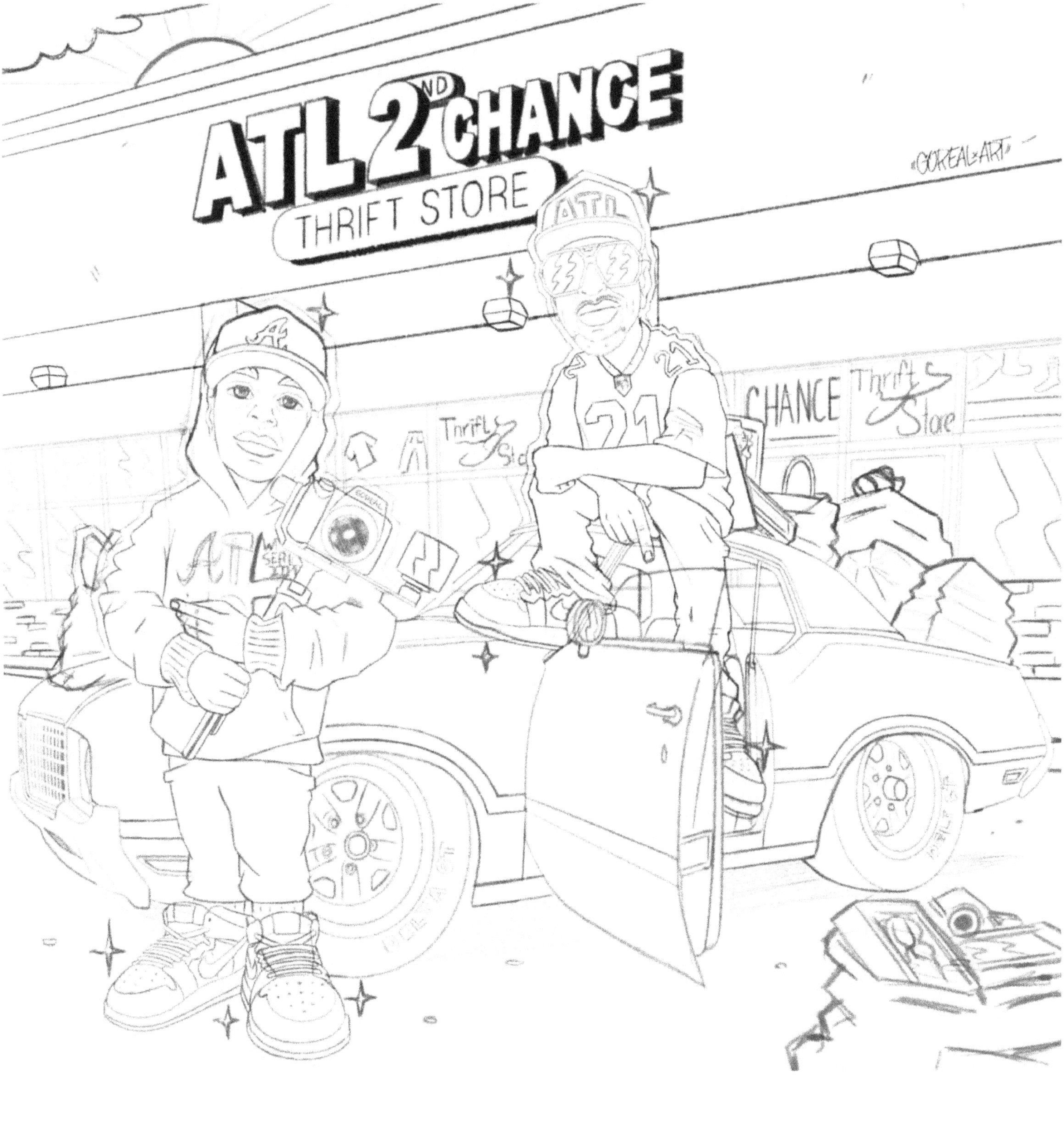
ATL 2ND CHANCE
THRIFT STORE
GOREAL ART
CHANCE
Thrift Store

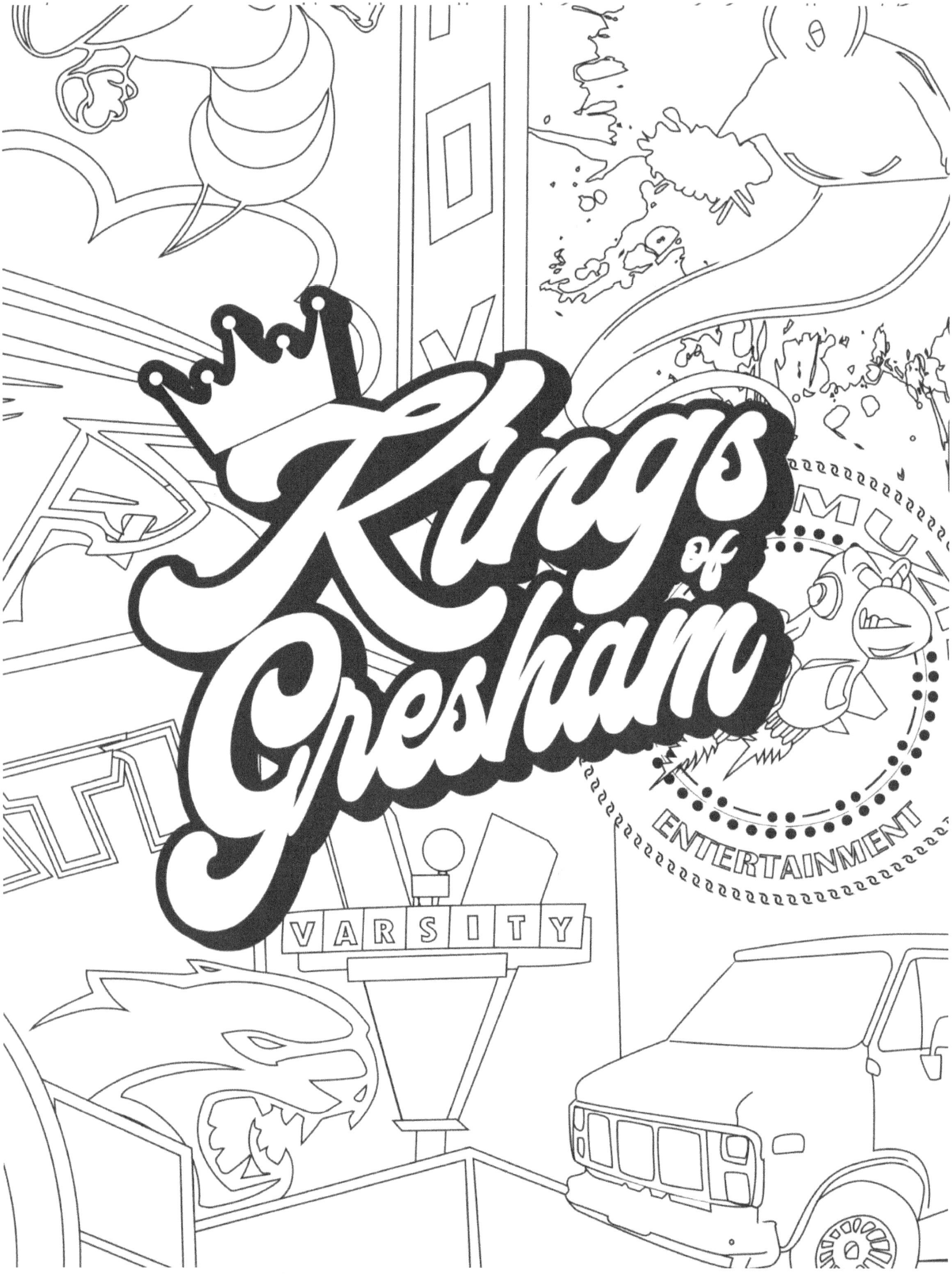
Kings of Gresham
ENTERTAINMENT
VARSITY

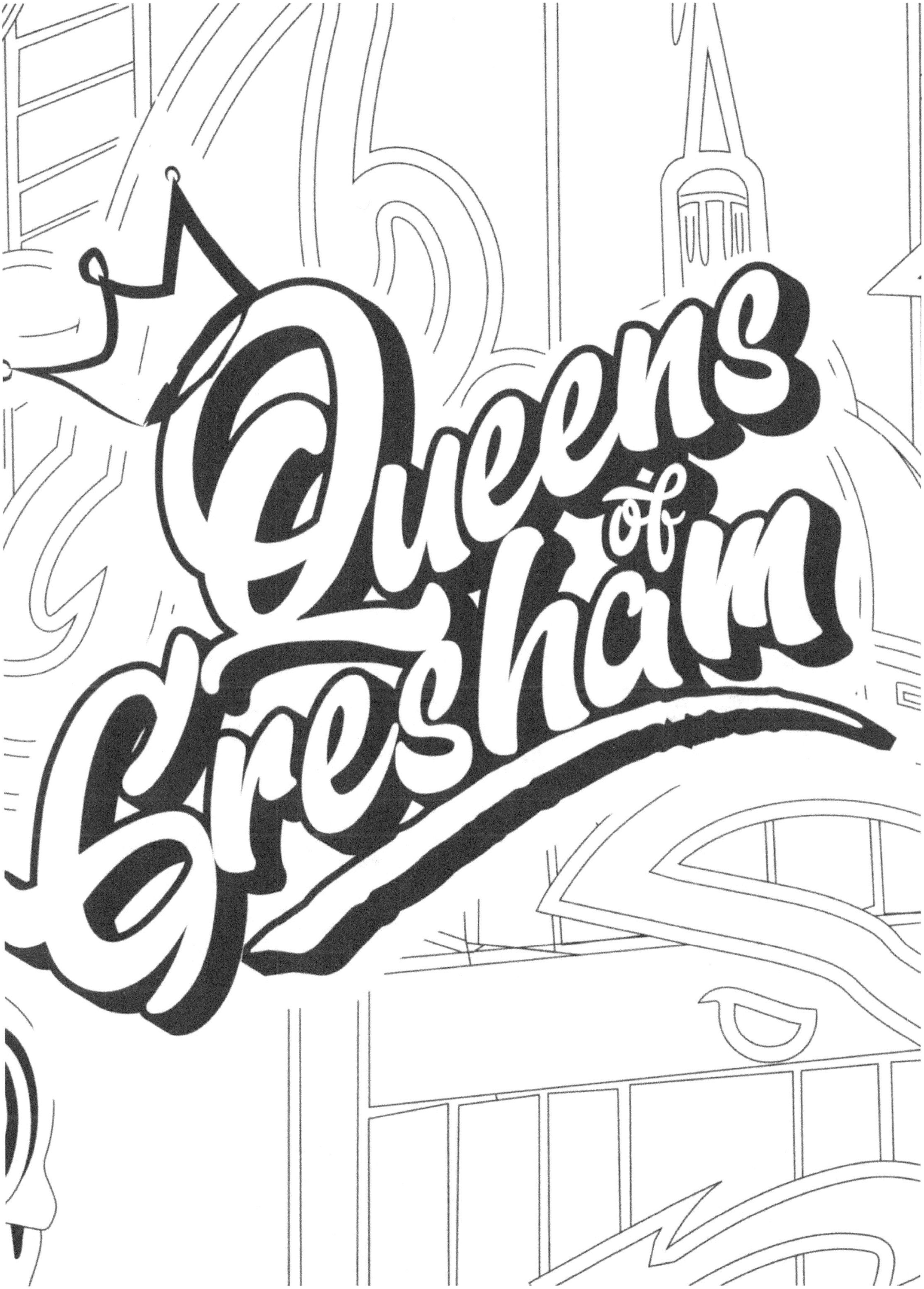
Queens
of
Gresham

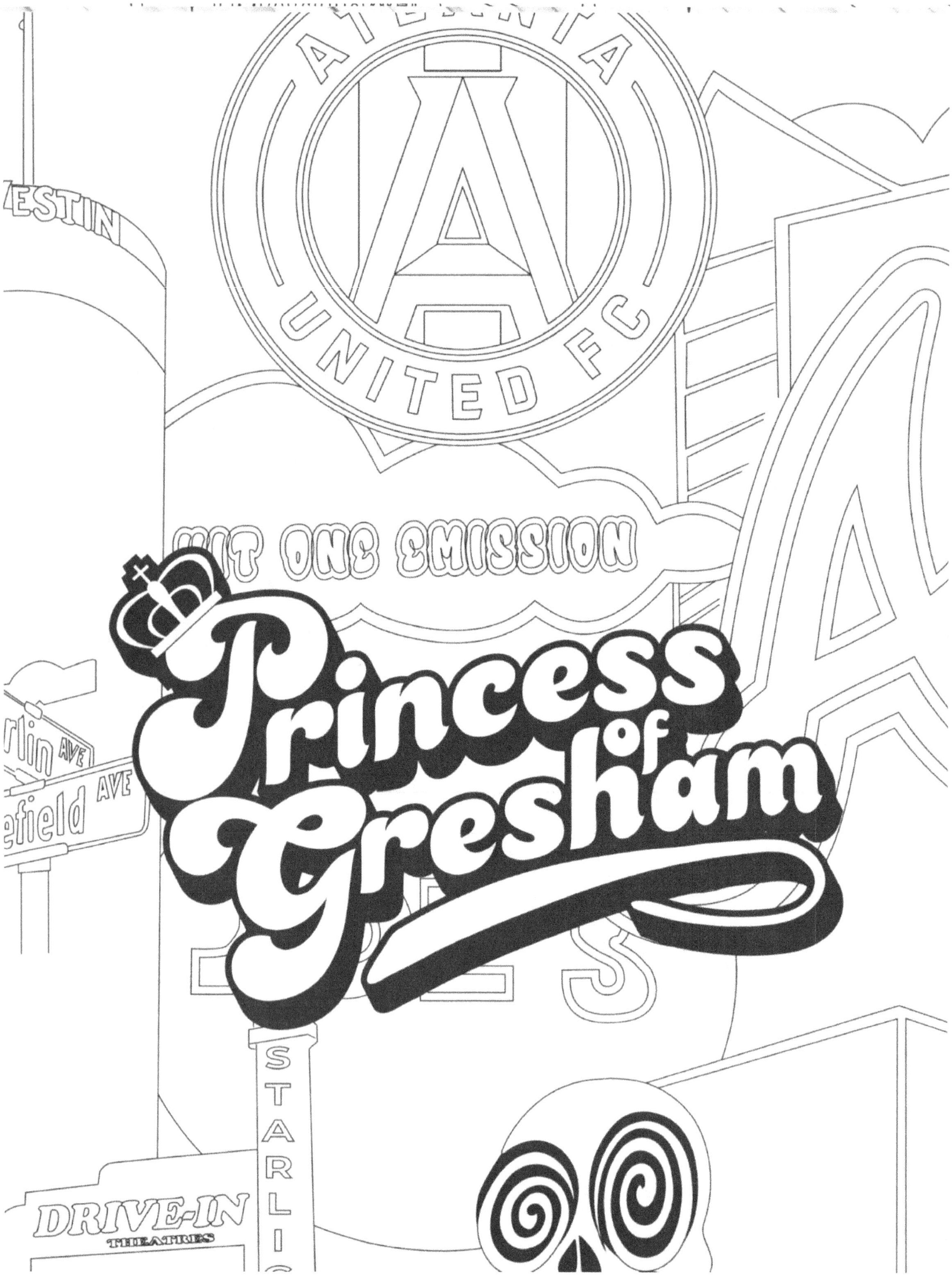

ATLANTA
UNITED FC
ONE EMISSION
Princess of Gresham
AVE
AVE
DRIVE-IN
THEATRES

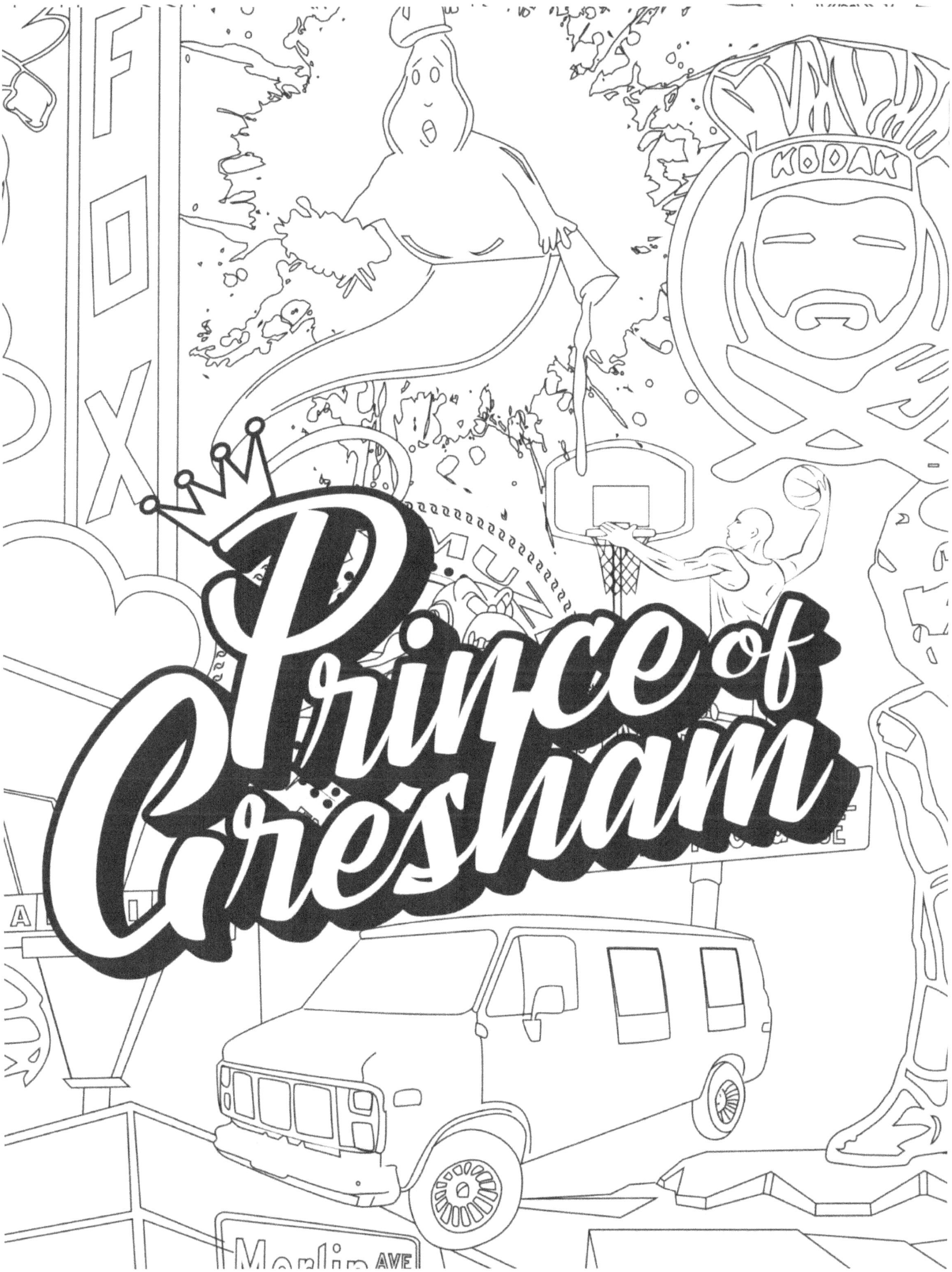
FOX
KODAK
Prince of Gresham
Merlin AVE

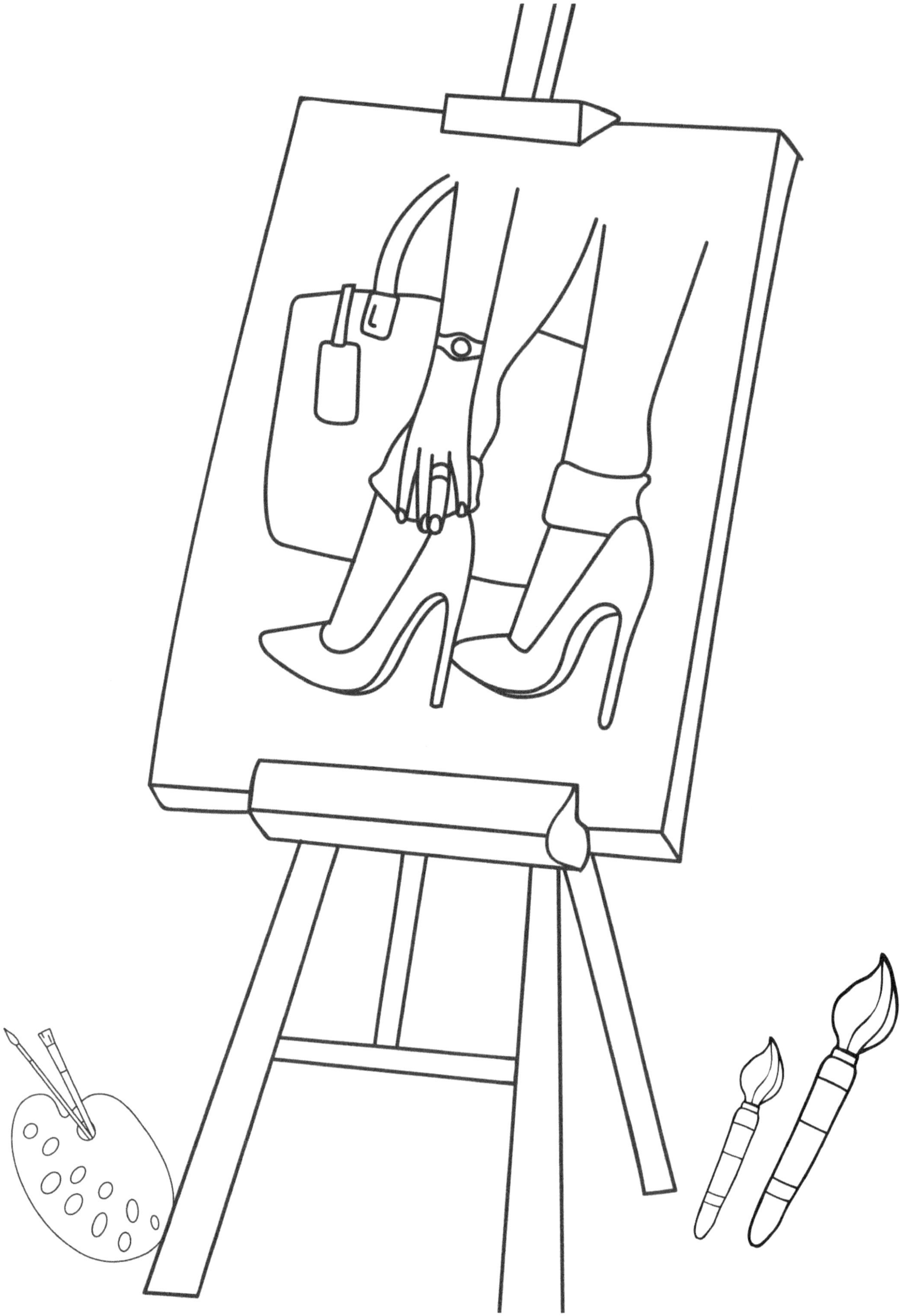

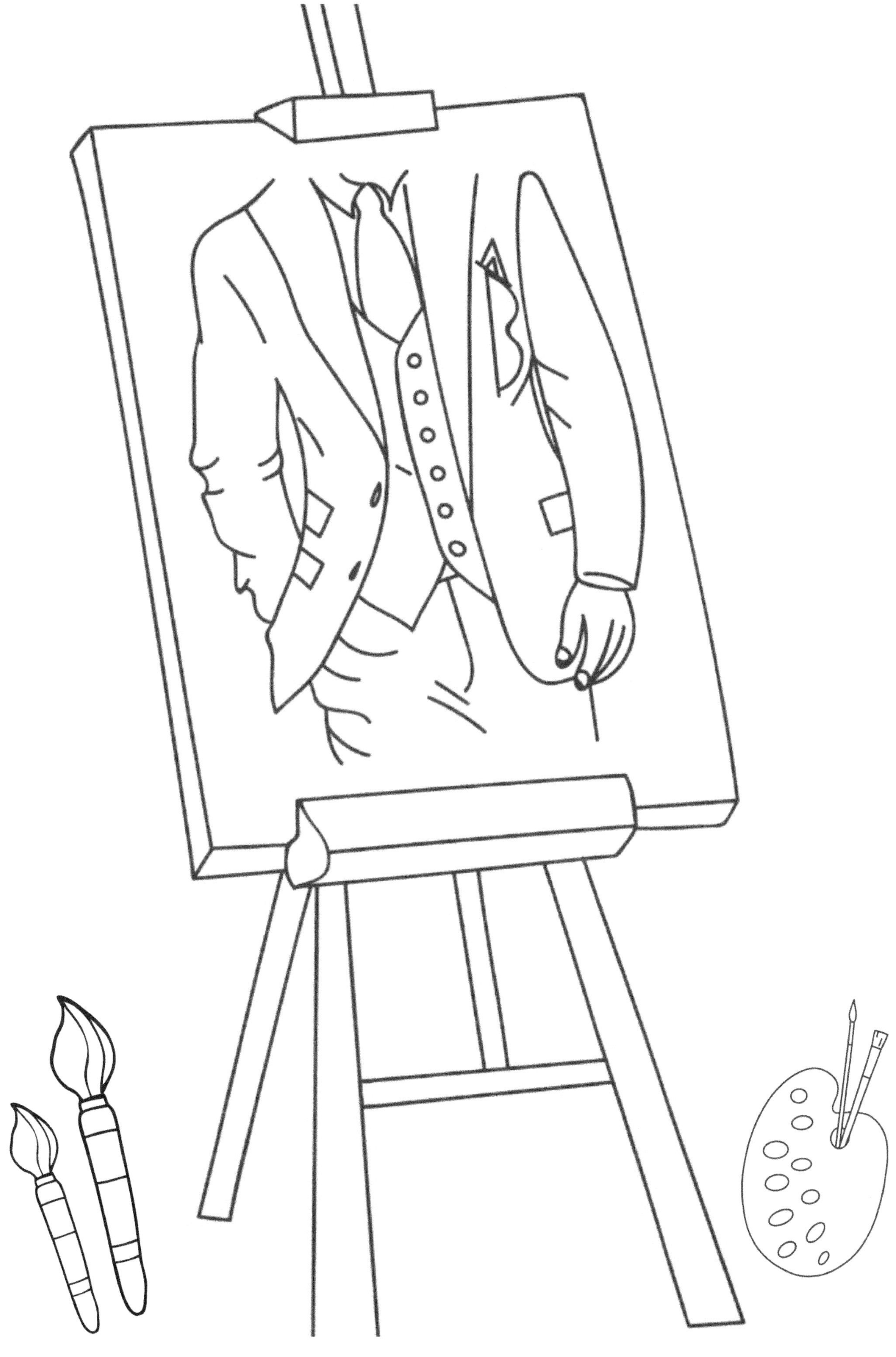

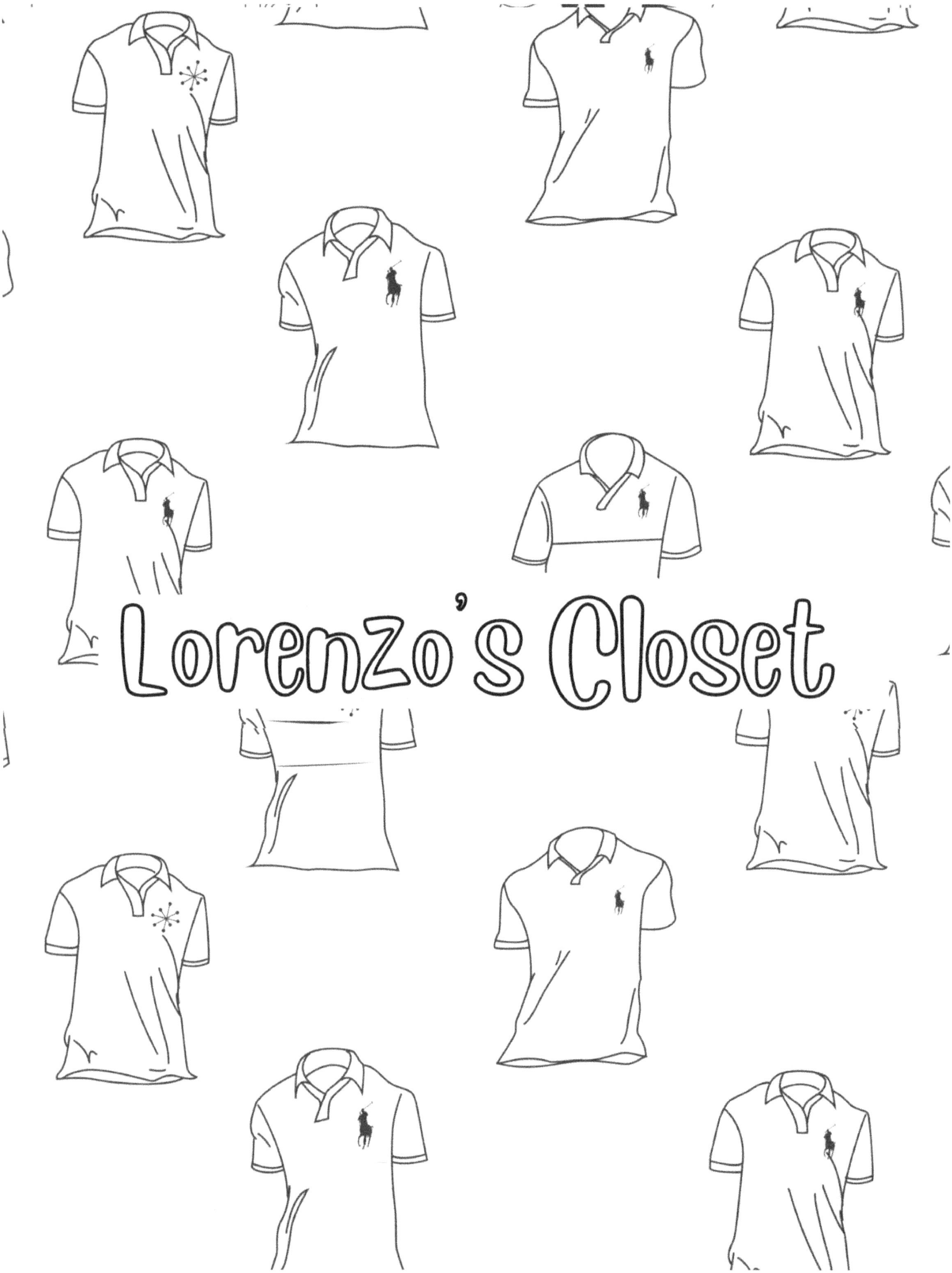
Lorenzo's Closet

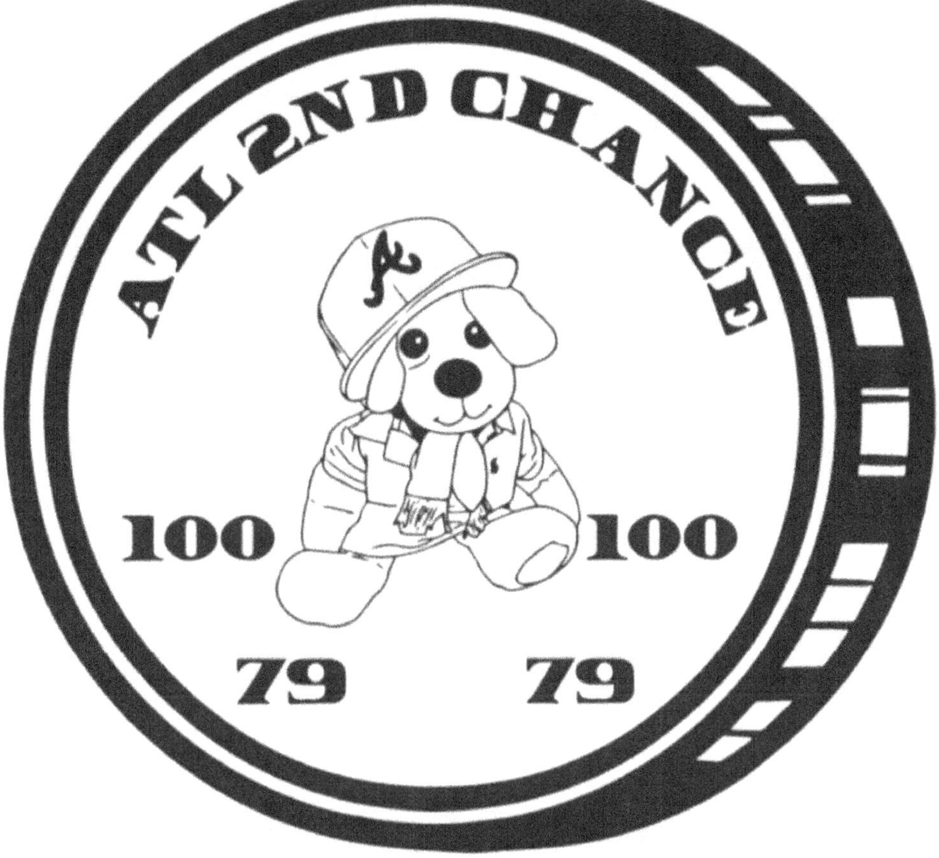
ATL 2ND CHANCE
100
100
79
79

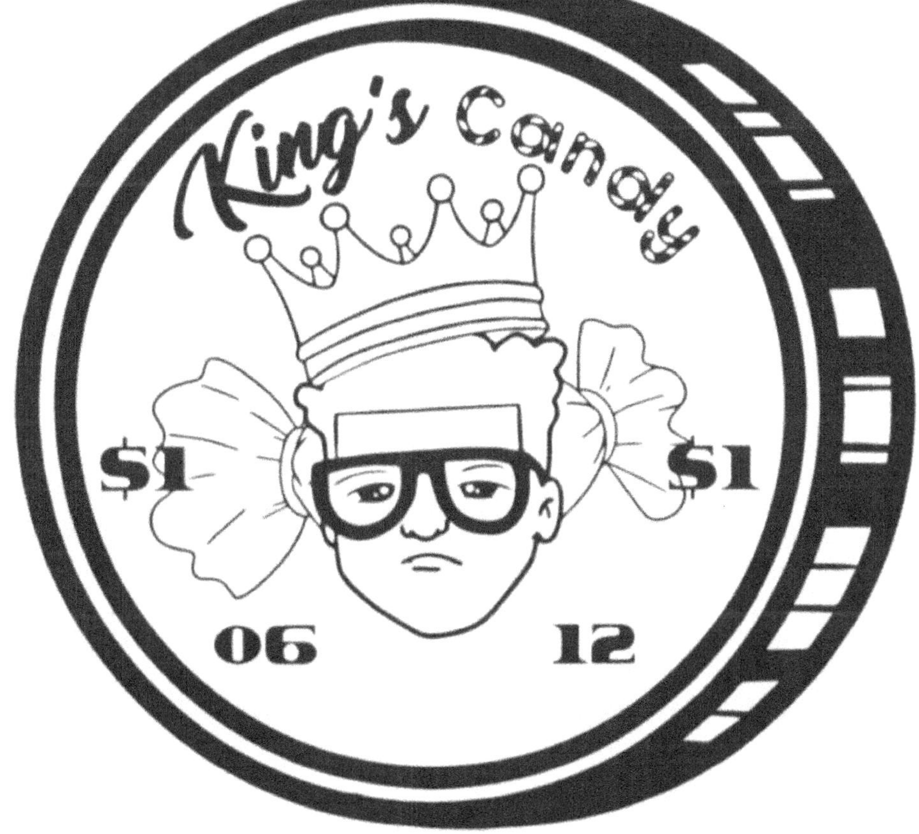
King's Candy
$1
$1
06
12

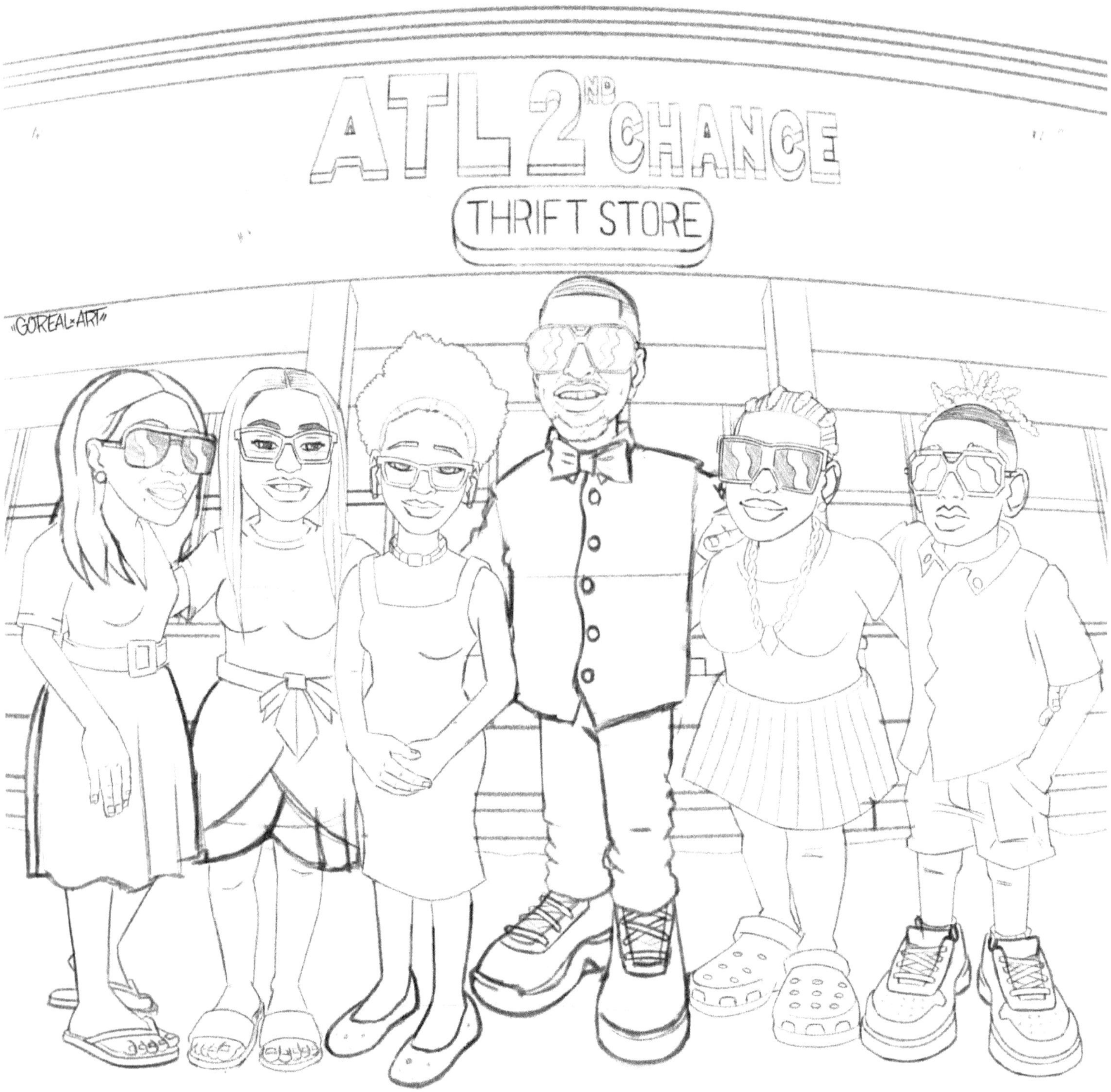

ATL 2ND CHANCE
THRIFT STORE
GOREAL ART

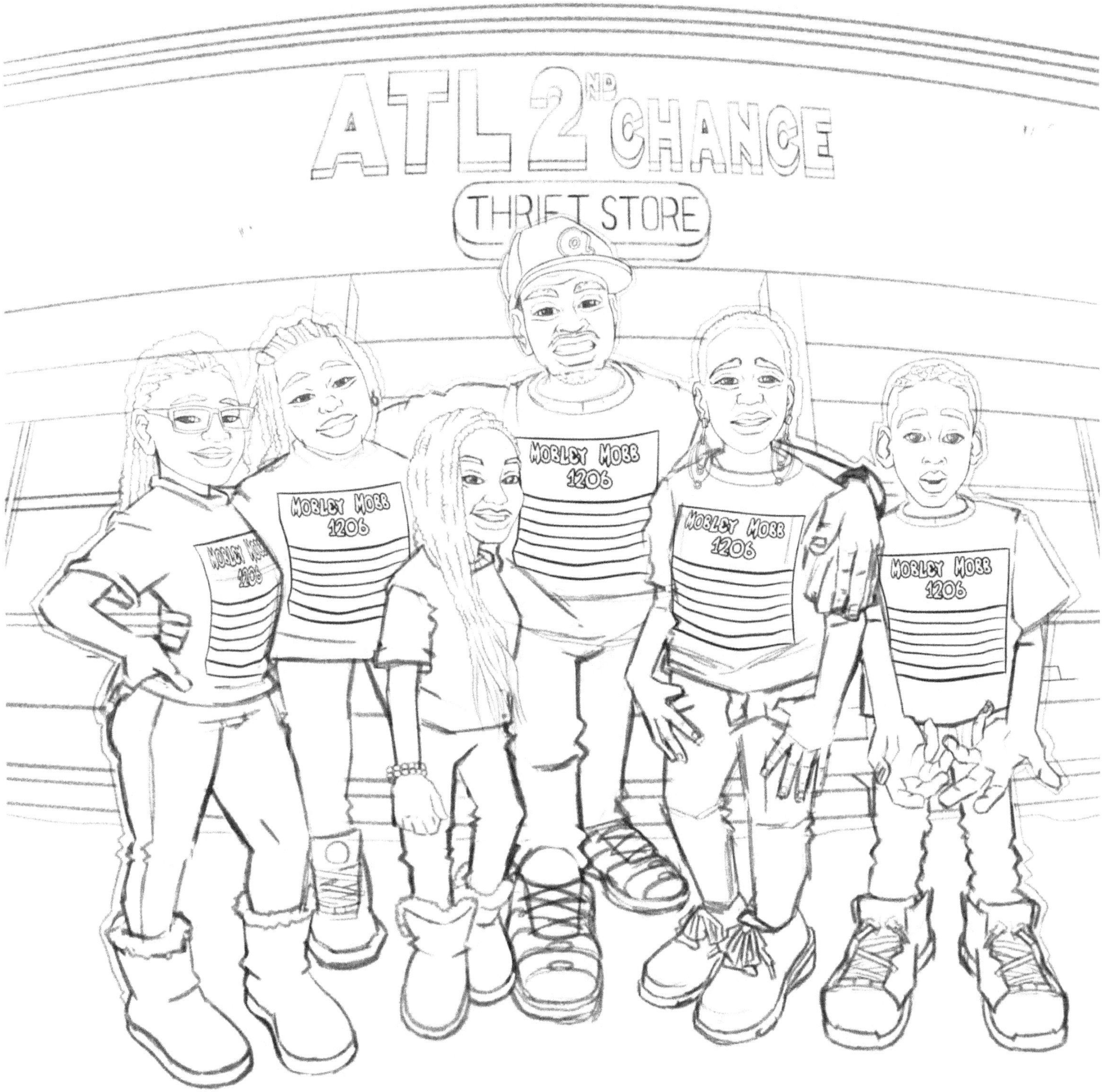
ATL 2ND CHANCE
THRIFT STORE
MOBLEY MOBB
1206
MOBLEY MOBB
1206
MOBLEY MOBB
1206
MOBLEY MOBB
1206
MOBLEY MOBB
1206

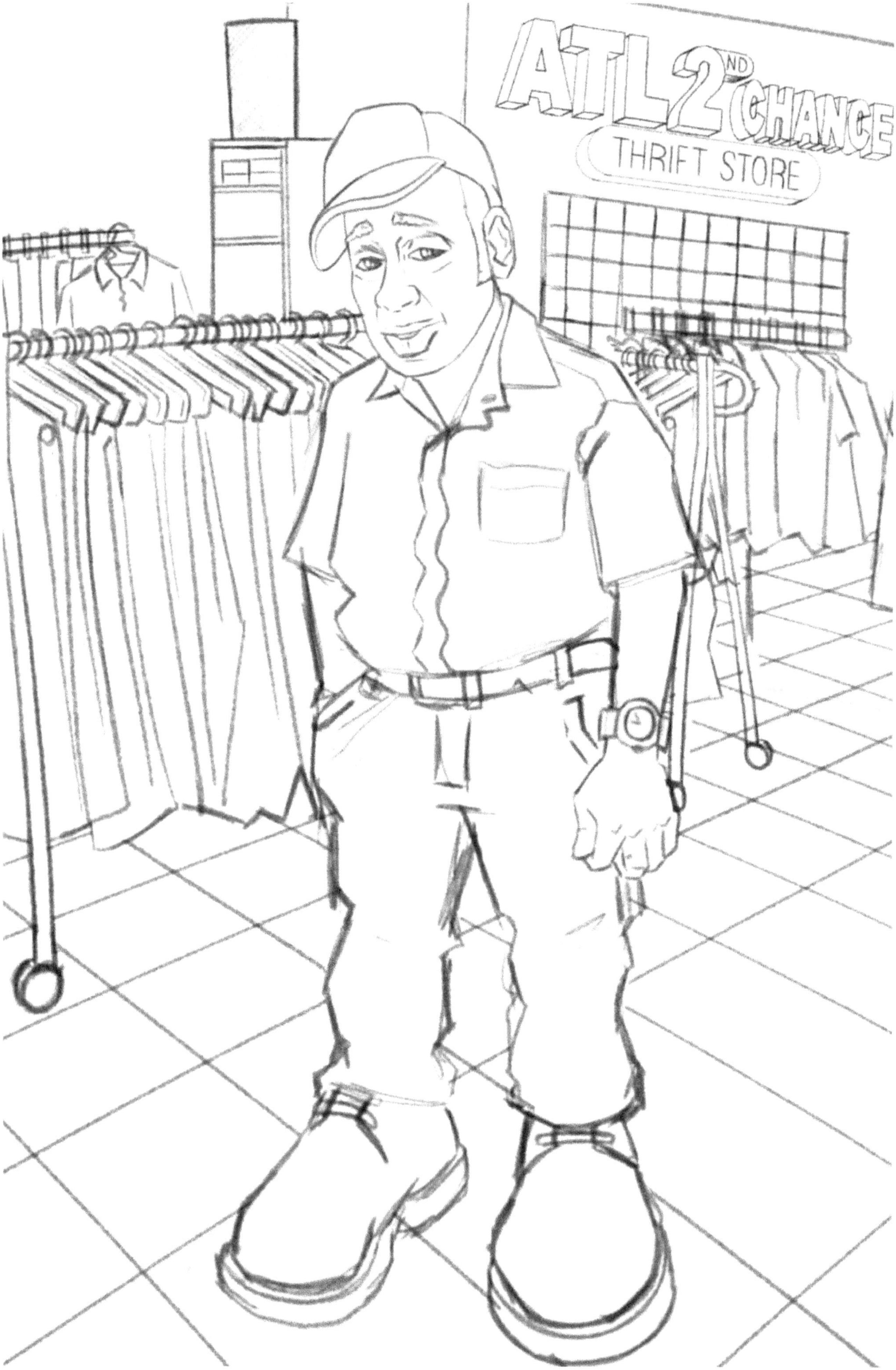
ATL 2ND CHANCE
THRIFT STORE

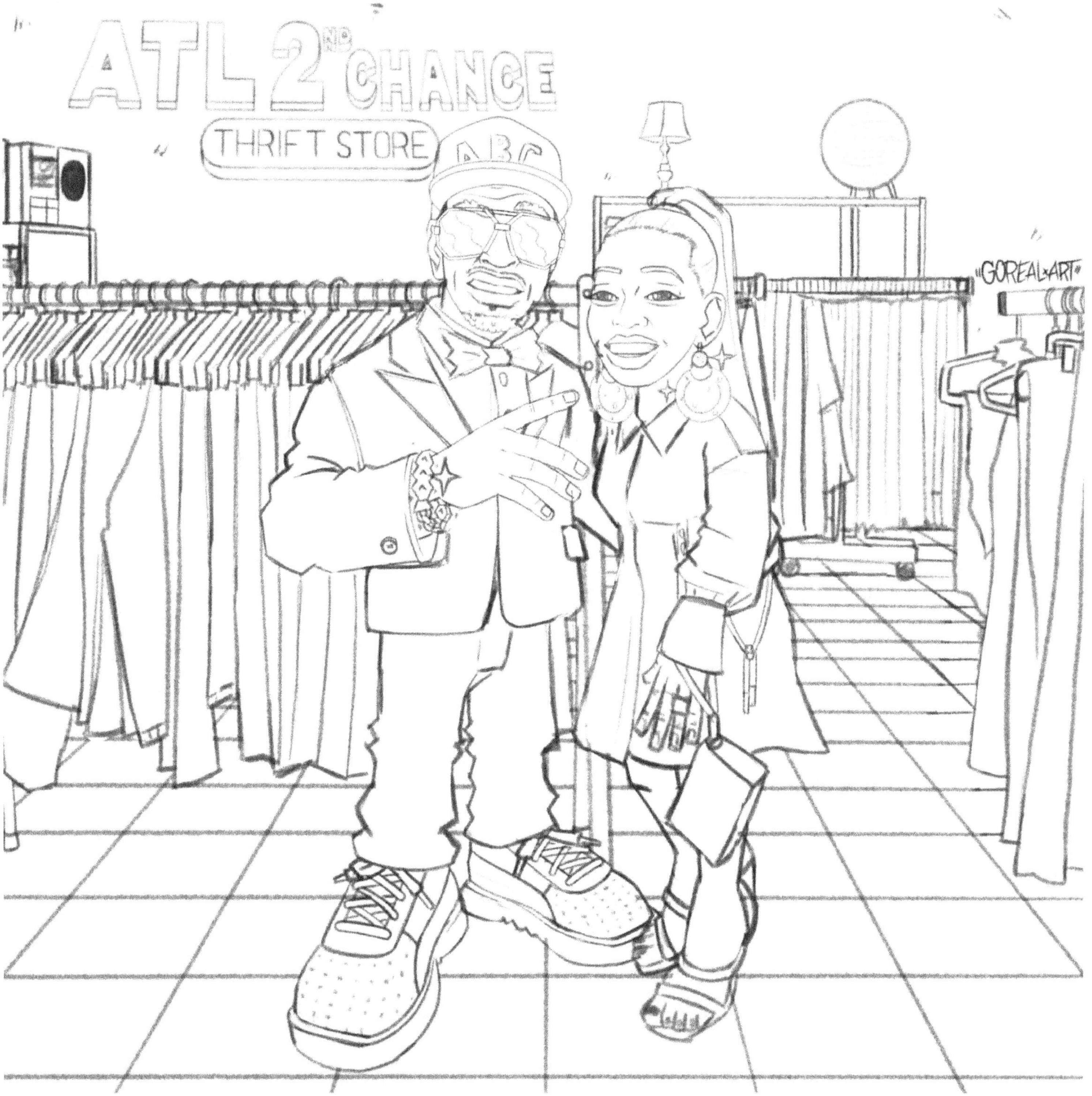
ATL 2ND CHANCE
THRIFT STORE
ABC
"GOREAL×ART"

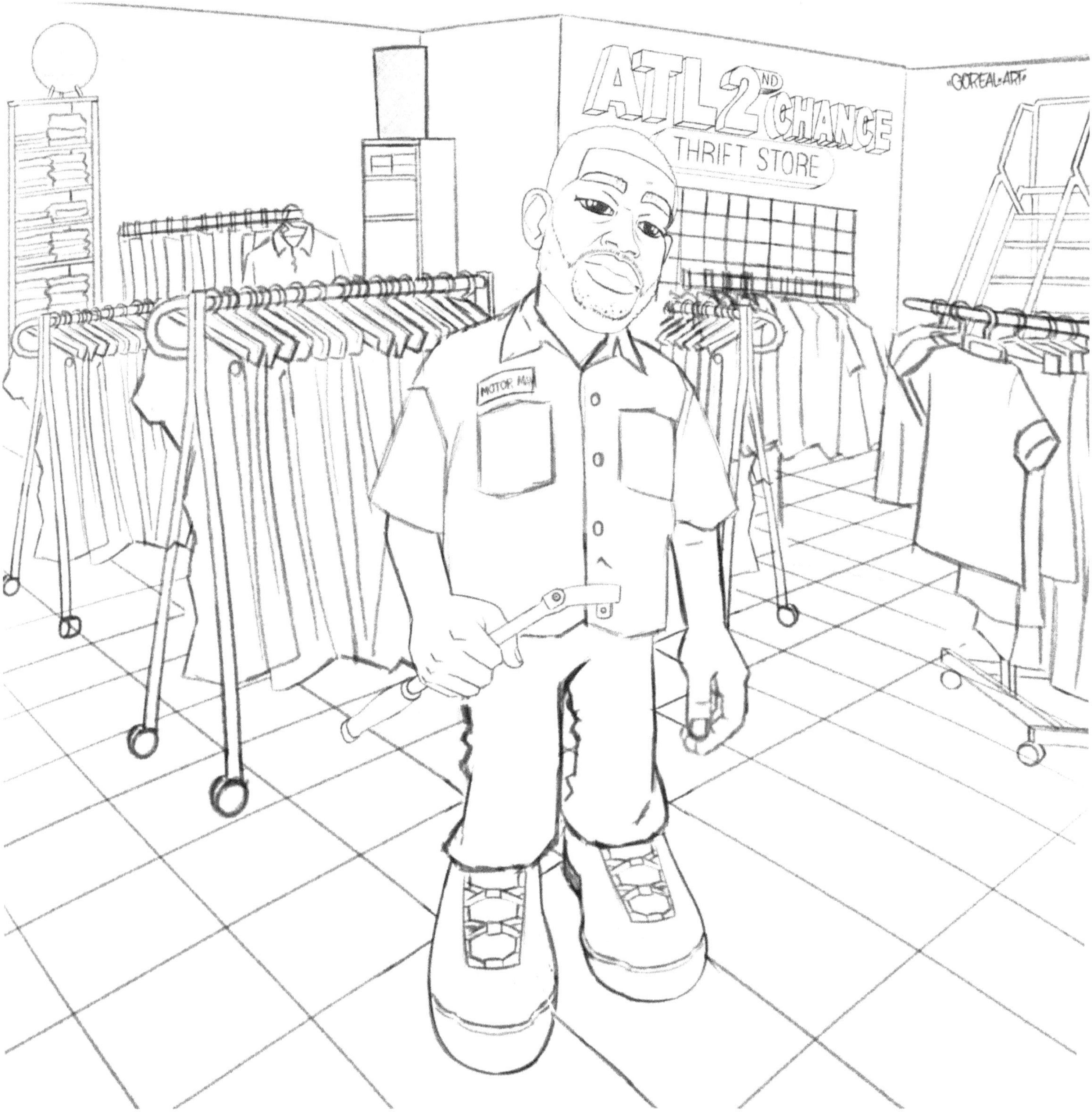
ATL 2ND CHANCE
THRIFT STORE
GOREAL ART

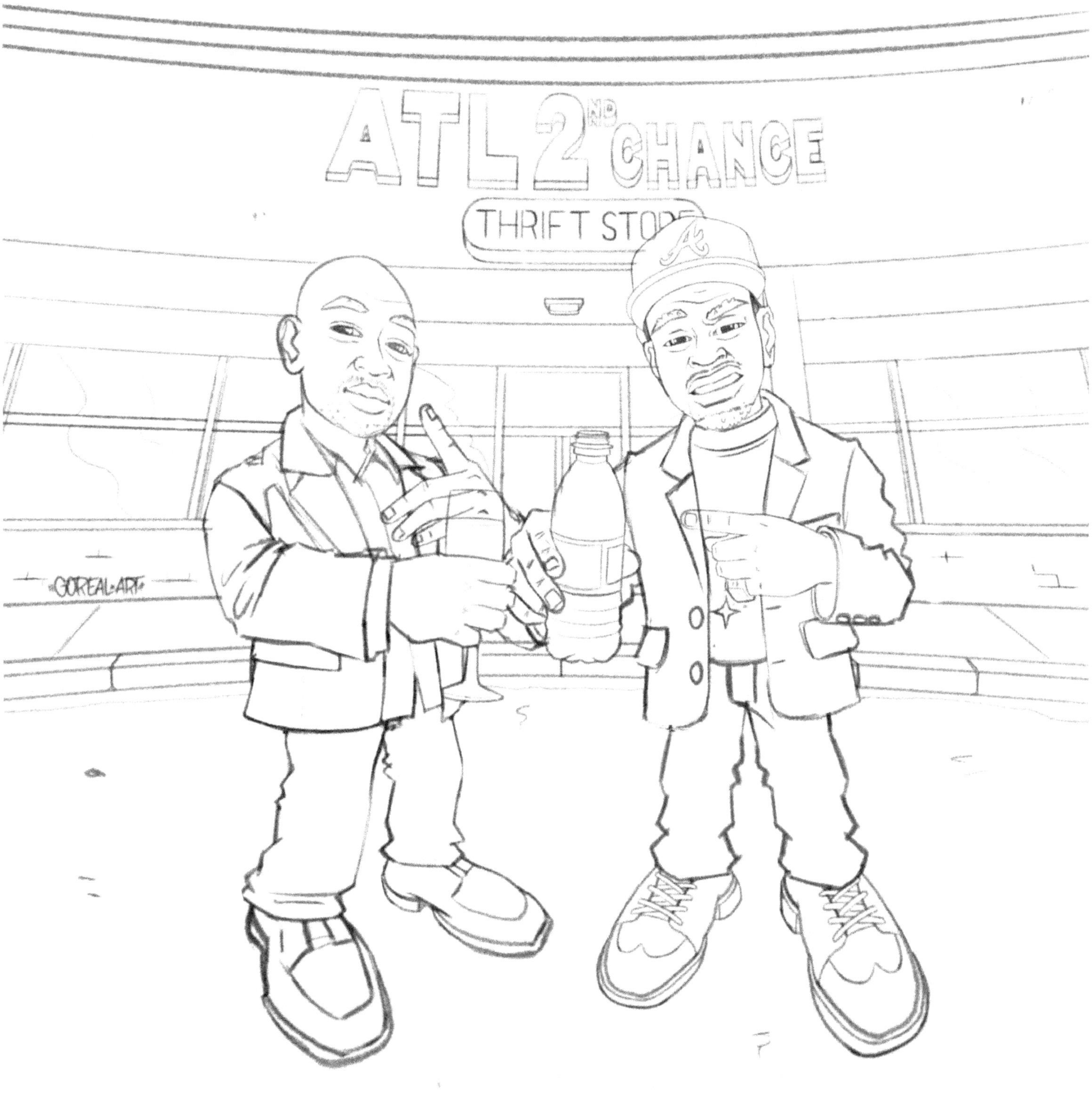

ATL 2ND CHANCE
THRIFT STORE
GOREAL ART

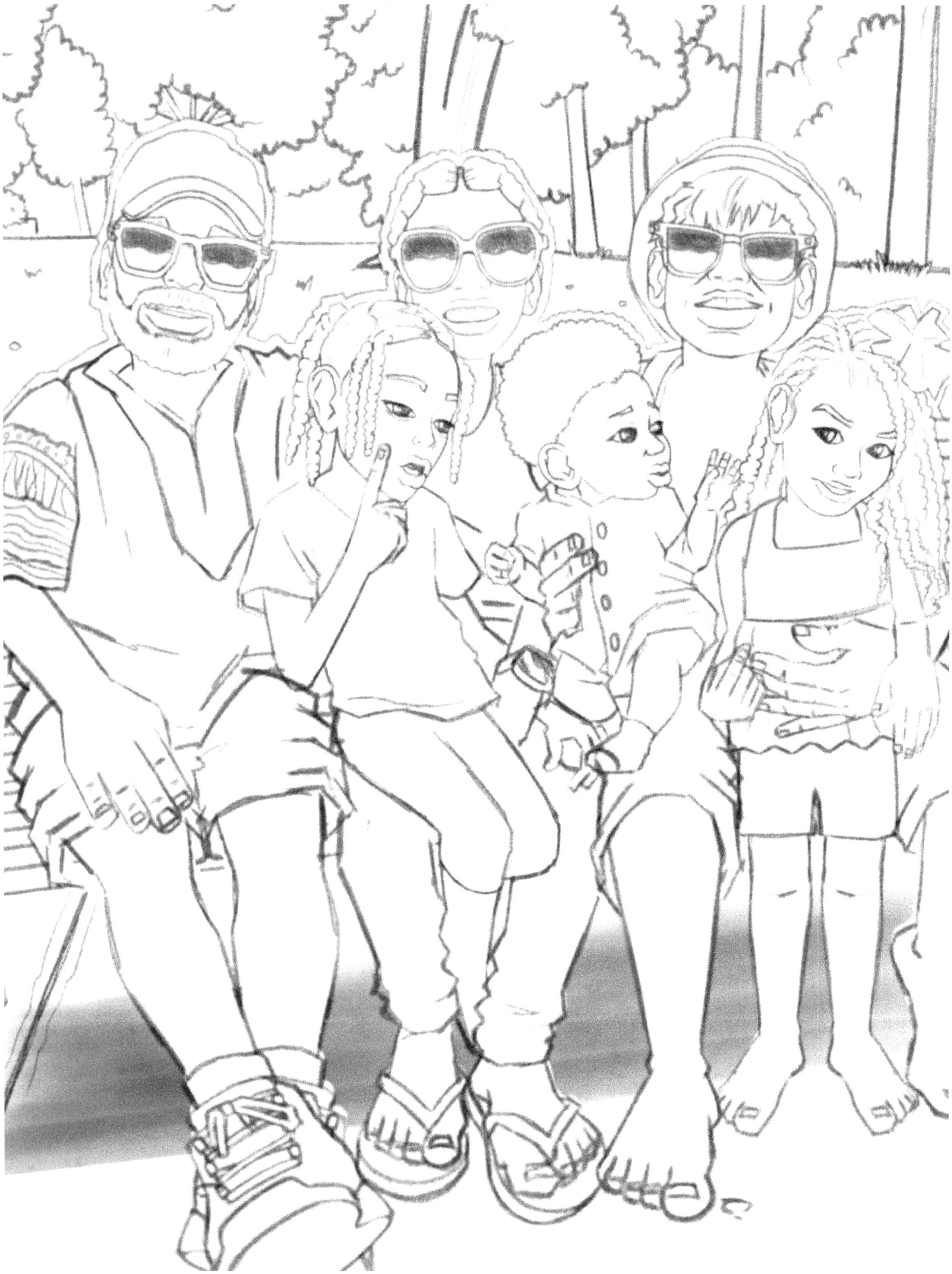

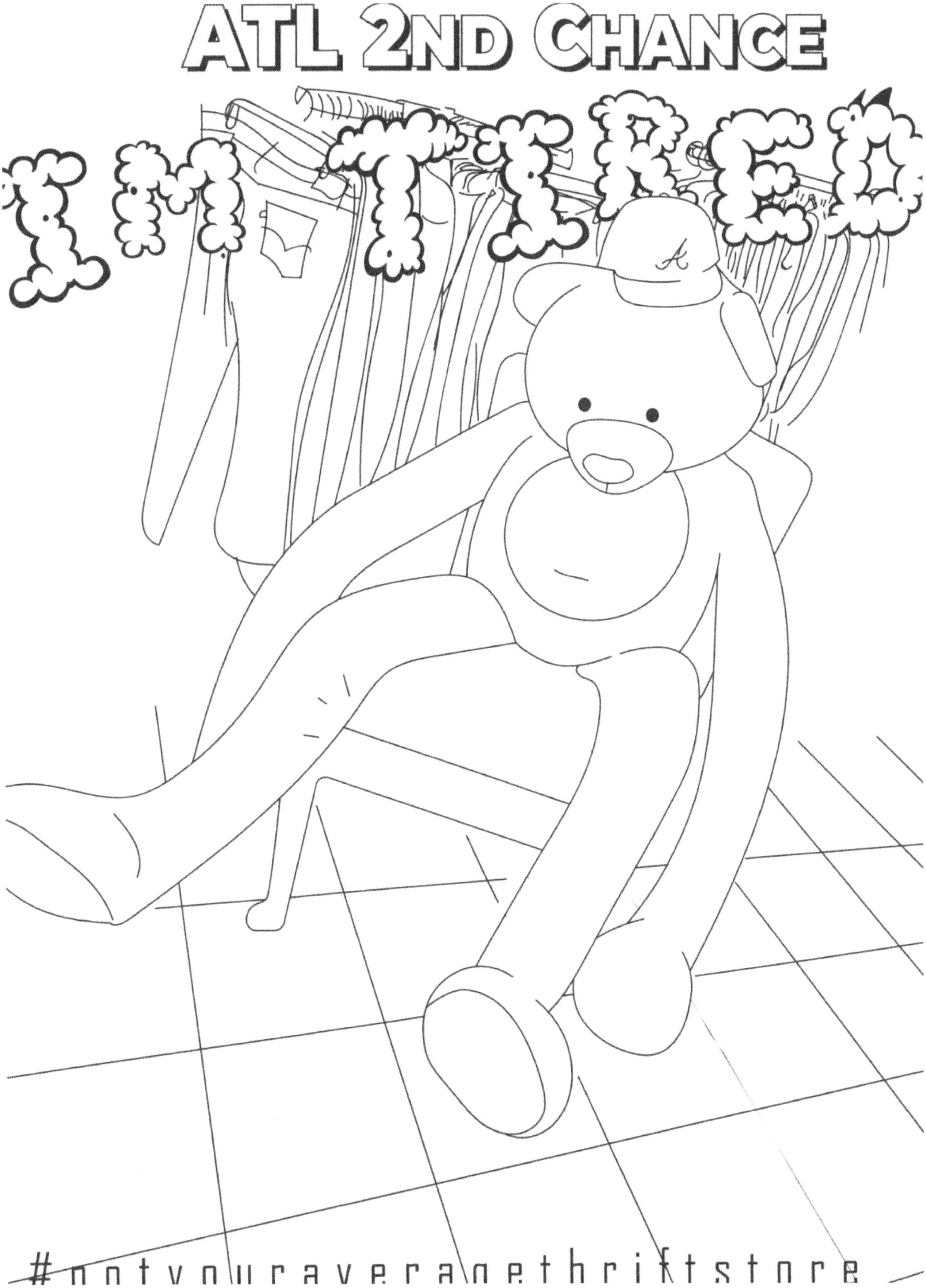
ATL 2ND CHANCE
I'M TIRED
#notyouraveragethriftstore

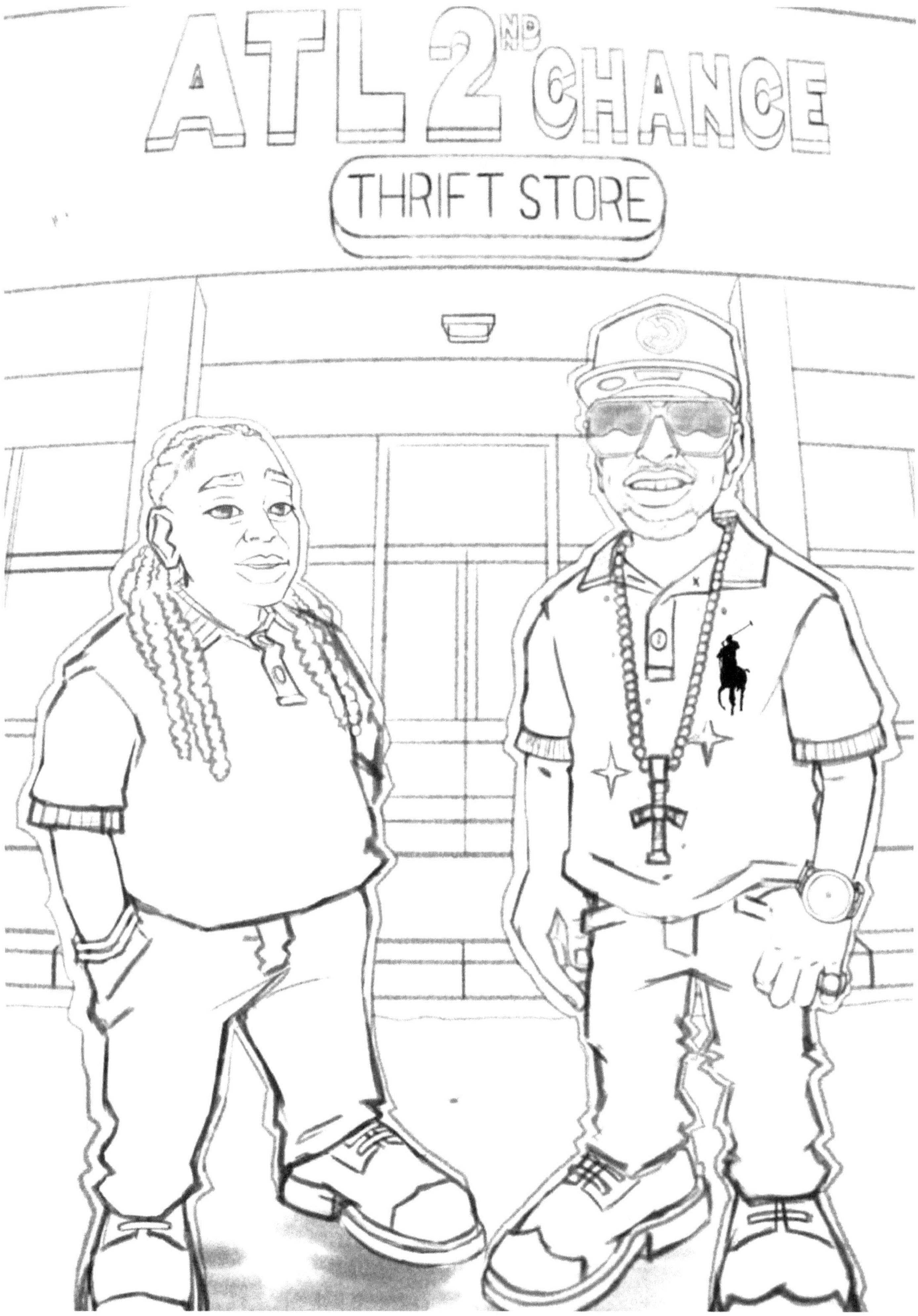
ATL 2ND CHANCE
THRIFT STORE

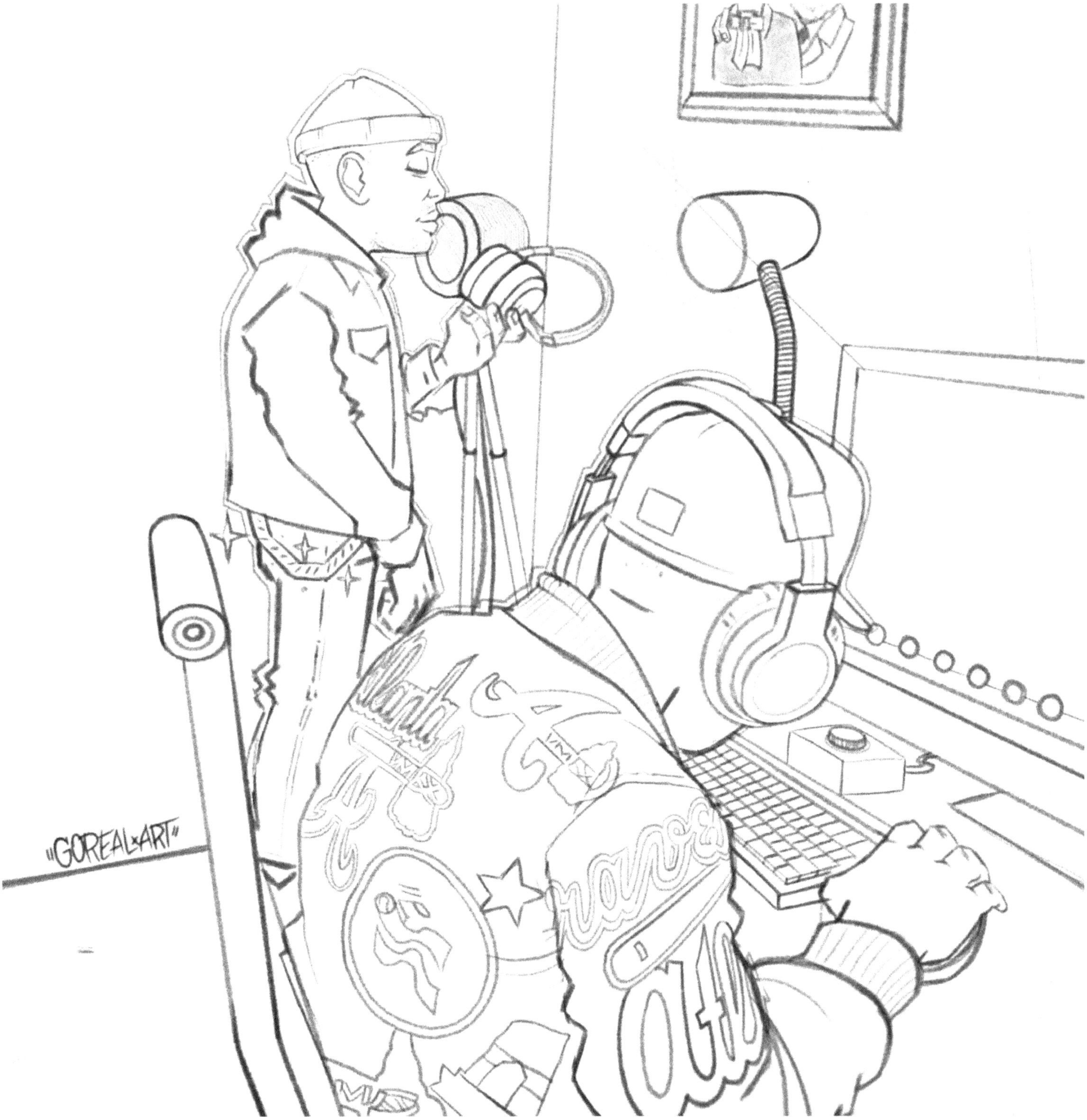
"GOREALxART"

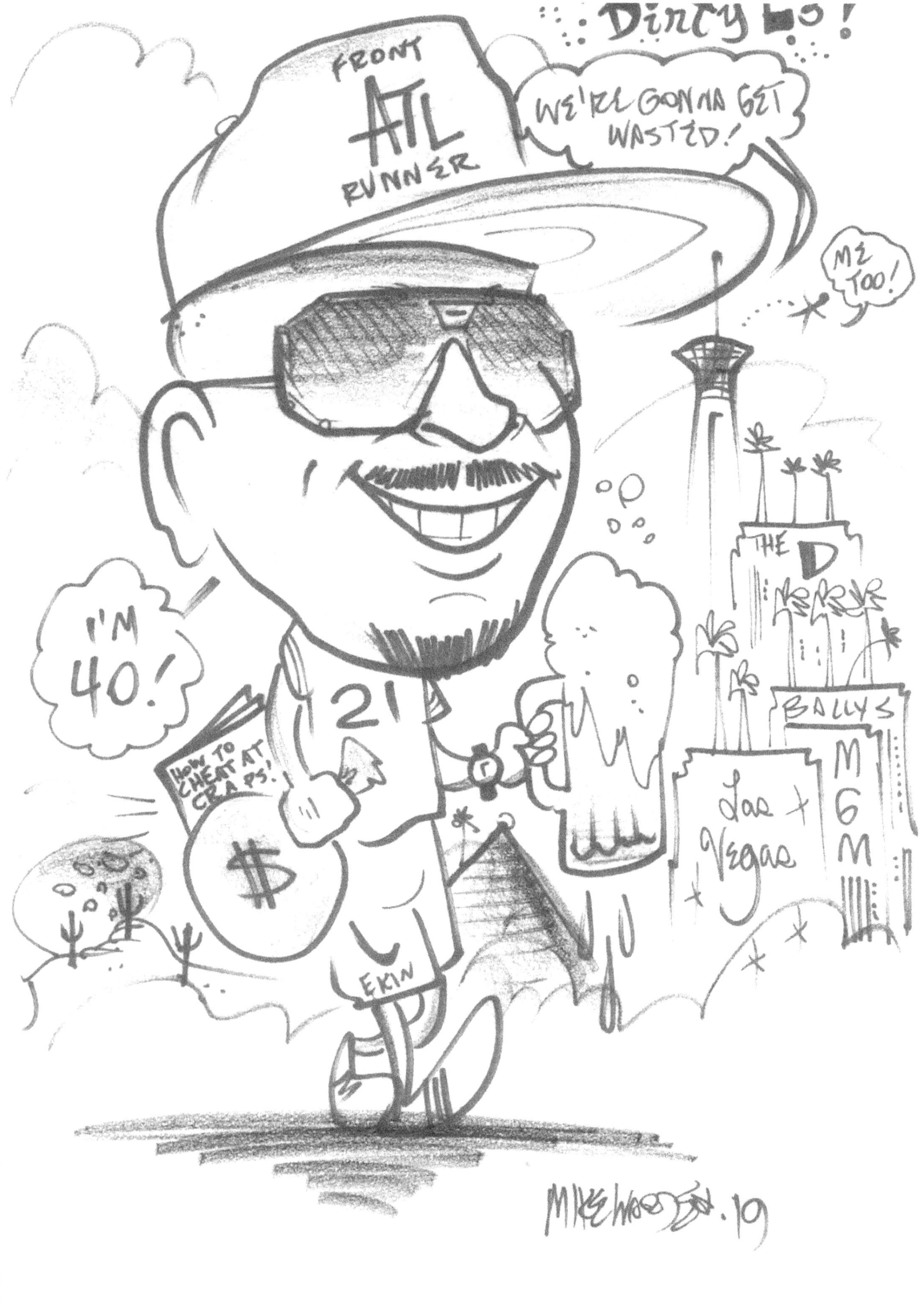

FRONT
ATL
RUNNER
WE'RE GONNA GET WASTED!
ME TOO!
I'M 40!
21
HOW TO CHEAT AT CRAPS!
$
EKIN
THE D
BALLYS
MGM
Las Vegas

www.ingramcontent.com/pod-product-compliance
Lightning Source LLC
Chambersburg PA
CBHW080439220526
45465CB00009B/3347
* 9 7 9 8 3 5 4 0 3 7 9 3 3 *